Alexander Skiba

The Bush-Administration's Iran Policy and Europe

Alexander Skiba

The Bush-Administration's Iran Policy and Europe

From «Regime Change» to «Engagement»?

VDM Verlag Dr. Müller

Imprint

Bibliographic information by the German National Library: The German National Library lists this publication at the German National Bibliography; detailed bibliographic information is available on the Internet at http://dnb.d-nb.de.

Cover image: www.purestockx.com

Publisher:
VDM Verlag Dr. Müller Aktiengesellschaft & Co. KG, Dudweiler Landstr. 125 a, 66123 Saarbrücken, Germany,
Phone +49 681 9100-698, Fax +49 681 9100-988,
Email: info@vdm-verlag.de

Produced in USA and UK by:
Lightning Source Inc., La Vergne, Tennessee, USA
Lightning Source UK Ltd., Milton Keynes, UK
BookSurge LLC, 5341 Dorchester Road, Suite 16, North Charleston, SC 29418, USA

ISBN: 978-3-8364-8773-3

To Grit and my parents.

Executive Summary

The United States and Europe have a long track record of seemingly irreconcilable approaches towards "rogue states." While Washington typically sought to isolate and punish countries like Iran, Europe preferred different forms of engagement. During the run-up to the Iraq War in 2003, the transatlantic relationship experienced its most dramatic deterioration since perhaps the Suez crisis. Overshadowed by these developments, Iran's nuclear ambitions emerged as a pressing strategic challenge with direct implications for transatlantic relations. While Germany, France and the UK (E3) started a diplomatic process of conditional engagement with Tehran, the Bush administration looked poised to clash with its allies over Iran policy. Indeed, during the years of 2003 and 2004 a common transatlantic approach seemed out of reach. After President Bush's re-election, however, U.S. Iran policy adjusted surprisingly in favor of supporting the European negotiation process. In May 2006, departing from its traditional opposition to engagement with "rogue states," Washington declared that it would even be ready to join multilateral talks with Iran and provide substantial economic incentives.

In this book I try to answer the question why American Iran policy has shifted towards supporting the European approach between the summer of 2003 and May 2006. I start by devising three different theoretical perspectives that allow for a focus on different aspects of the issue: The first angle, drawn from neorealist premises, highlights the larger context of U.S. foreign policy and emphasizes the structural constraints under which it was formulated. A complementary liberal perspective (called Liberalism I) draws attention to the polyarchic nature of the Bush administration – i.e. the different centers of power impacting the formulation of U.S. foreign policy – and emphasizes the concentration of presidential power and the growing influence of the State Department on Iran policy after President Bush's reelection in 2005 and 2006. A second liberal viewpoint (Liberalism II) allows us to look at U.S. Iran policy from a transatlantic angle: This perspective showcases how Germany attempted to influence Washington's position on Iran between 2003 and 2006.

As the analysis shows, the Bush administration was unable to formulate an autonomous–i.e. unilateral–Iran policy according to its original policy preference of containing and isolating Iran at the outset of the nuclear crisis in 2003. The U.S. had to revise this preference as it was faced with a lack of good military options and a rapid decline of influence around the world in the aftermath of the Iraq War. The dysfunctional make-up of the Bush administration's national security policy team prohibited meaningful changes in favor of multilateral diplomacy during President Bush's first term. But personnel changes in the second administration—most notably the promotion of Condoleezza Rice as Secretary of State—allowed for gradual adjustments. The shifts in U.S. Iran policy in the direction of the European approach in 2005 and 2006 can be best explained by a combination of three factors: First, America's freedom of action was limited following the Iraq War. Second, the streamlining process within President Bush's foreign policy staff set the stage for gradual policy adjustments. Third, the growing influence of Germany, especially after the election of Angela Merkel as Federal Chancellor—as a part of the E3—on the process of formulating U.S. Iran policy facilitated transatlantic policy coordination towards Iran.

List of Abbreviations

E3 .... European Three (Germany, France, United Kingdom)

EU .... European Union

GDP .... Gross Domestic Product

IAEA .... International Atomic Energy Agency

IR .... International Relations

MEK .... Mujahedeen-e-Khalq (Iranian dissident group)

NAM .... Non-Aligned Movement

NATO .... North Atlantic Treaty Organization

NPT .... Nuclear Non-Proliferation Treaty

NSC .... National Security Council

NSPD .... National Security Presidential Directive

SCIRI .... Supreme Council for Islamic Revolution in Iraq

TCA .... EU Trade and Cooperation Agreement

UK .... United Kingdom

UN .... United Nations

U.S. .... United States

WMD .... Weapons of Mass Destruction

Table of Contents

A.   Introduction and Overview 6

   1.   Transatlantic Relations and "Rogue States:" A Tug-of-War.. 6

   2.   Empirical Puzzle and Research Question 9

   3.   The Dependent Variable: Adjustments of U.S. Iran Policy... 12

   4.   Theoretical Framework.. 16

      4.1.   Neorealist Foreign Policy Theory *17*

      4.2.   Liberal Foreign Policy Theory I *21*

      4.3.   Liberal Foreign Policy Theory II... *23*

   5.   Methodology, Sourcing and Structure 26

B.   Three Perspectives on U.S. Iran Policy 29

   1.   Neorealism: Power on the Wane.. 29

      1.1.   Decline of U.S. Military, Economic and Political Power? *30*

      1.2.   An Emboldened and More Powerful Iran.. *33*

      1.3.   Analysis of U.S. Iran Policy (2003-2004) *33*

      1.4.   Analysis of U.S. Iran Policy (2005-2006) *37*

      1.5.   Summary.. *41*

   2.   Liberalism I: The Two Bush Administrations.. 42

      2.1.   Main Players in the First Bush Administration *44*

      2.2.   Analysis of U.S. Iran Policy (2003-2004) *47*

      2.3.   Main Players in the Second Bush Administration... *53*

      2.4.   Analysis of U.S. Iran Policy (2005-2006) *55*

      2.5.   Summary.. *60*

   3.   Liberalism II: The Influence of Germany.. 62

      3.1.   Introduction to German Iran Policy *62*

      3.2.   The First Bush Administration (2003-2004)... *63*

      3.3.   The Second Bush Administration (2005-2006).. *68*

      3.4.   Summary.. *73*

C.   Conclusion and Outlook 75

   1.   Solving the Empirical Puzzle 75

   2.   Iran and Future Transatlantic Policy Coordination... 78

Bibliography 80

"The future of the German-American relationship will not be founded on sentiment, friendship or common values, but rather on the cold calculation of self-interest. [...] The key question for the future is whether the common strategic interests that remain can be shaped to give the relationship a realistic basis."[1]

A. Introduction and Overview

1. Transatlantic Relations and "Rogue States:" A Tug-of-War

After the Soviet threat vanished in the early 90s, American and European policy makers, scholars and pundits engaged in a fiery debate about how to cope with individual countries that could pose security challenges to the international community in the future. Although the United States and Europe had disagreed over trading with Moscow during the Cold War era, they had still shared the overarching goal of containing the Soviets. The fundamental agreement on the premises of *containment* policy set clear limits on cooperation with the East and guaranteed that transatlantic unity would not be put into jeopardy in times of crisis.[2]

As potentially hostile states—such as Iraq, Iran and North Korea—multiplied, a strategically sound transatlantic agreement over how threatening these states were and how to handle them had to be found anew. Even agreeing on common language, however, proved to be an elusive task.[3] In 1994, Anthony Lake, President Clinton's National Security Advisor, framed the debate from a U.S. point of view.

"[O]ur policy must face the reality of recalcitrant and outlaw states that not only choose to remain outside the family but also assault its basic values. There are few "backlash" states: Cuba, North Korea, Iran, Iraq and Libya."[4]

---

[1]   Stephen F. Szabo, *Parting Ways. The crisis in German-American Relations* (Washington, DC: Brookings Press, 2005) 140.

[2]   Cf. Charles Lane, "Germany's New Ostpolitik," *Foreign Affairs* 74, no. 6, November/December (1994) 77-89.

[3]   For a good discussion of transatlantic differences with regard to the perception of 'Rogue States' see: Holger Stritzel, "German and American Perceptions of 'Rogue States'," *AICGS Advisor*, no. 13 October (2006).

[4]   Anthony Lake, "Confronting Backlash States," *Foreign Affairs* 74, no. 2, March/April (1994) 45-55.

From the American perspective, 'backlash states'—or 'rogue states,' as they were later called—lacked the ability to engage constructively with the outside world: Ruled by autocratic regimes, these states held fervent ambitions to obtain weapons of mass destruction (WMD).[5]

Where Washington spotted clear and present danger, Europe saw a mix of risks and opportunities.[6] From a European point of view, stigmatizing individual states as innately 'rogue' ran contrary to every effort to help them integrate into the 'family of nations.' From these different perceptions flowed different policies: In opposition to 'containment and isolation,' Europe favored 'engagement and dialogue' as well as carefully targeted policies which would support a gradual transformation of "backlash states."[7]

More recently, these decade-old disagreements were overshadowed by a sobering re-evaluation of transatlantic affairs. During the run-up to the Iraq War in 2003, the U.S. and Europe experienced the most dramatic deterioration in their partnership since perhaps the Suez crisis.[8] While disagreements about proper rhetoric have continued, the practical question of how to forge a common approach towards states of concern has never been more acute. As Eberhard Sandschneider has argued conclusively, the unruly post-Cold War world saw a multiplication of security risks and challenges while satisfying transatlantic answers are still lacking.[9] The current state of transatlantic affairs is aptly summarized by Stephen Szabo's quote above: Only the formulation of common strategic interests will enable both sides of the Atlantic to cooperate successfully in the future.[10]

This book will take a closer look at tentative developments which point towards increased transatlantic policy coordination: Chiefly driven by policy adjustments in Washington, the United States and Europe have considerably narrowed their policy differences on Iran and its nuclear ambitions between 2003 and 2006. Against the backdrop of the traditionally irreconcilable

---

[5] Ibid.

[6] Peter Rudolf, "Stigmatisierung bestimmter Staaten. Europa bevorzugt den Dialog," *Internationale Politik*, no. 6 (1999) 15-22. For good introductions into the debate on "states of risk" see: Sven Behrendt, "Reintegration und Prävention von „Risikostaaten"," *Internationale Politik*, no. 6 (1999) 29-34, Christopher Daase, Susanne Feske, and Ingo Peters, eds., *Internationale Risikopolitik. Der Umgang mit neuen Gefahren in den internationalen Beziehungen* (Baden Baden: Nomos, 2002), Gerald Schneider and Patricia A. Weitsman, "Eliciting Collaboration From „Risky" States: The Limits of Conventional Multilateralism in Security Affairs," *Global Society* 11, no. 1 (January 1997) 93-110.

[7] For a good overview of different transatlantic approaches towards nuclear nonproliferation see: Harald Müller, "Nukleare Krisen und transatlantischer Dissens. Amerikanische und europäische Antworten auf aktuelle Probleme der Weiterverbreitung von Kernwaffen," in *HSFK Report* (Frankfurt am Main: Hessische Stiftung Friedens- und Konfliktforschung, September 2003).

[8] For a judgment to that effect see for example: Joshua William Busby, *Veto Powers and Political Distance in the Western Alliance* 2004 [12 June 2006]; available from wws.princeton.edu/jbusby/papers/apsa2004.pdf.

[9] Eberhard Sandschneider, "Reinventing Transatlantic Relations," in *AICGS/DAAD Working Paper Series* (Washington, DC: AICGS, 2003).

[10] For an excellent overview on contentious issues in transatlantic relations and their perception on both sides of the Atlantic see: Ingo Peters, "Introduction: Contending Versions and Competing Visions of Transatlantic Relations," in *Transatlantic Tug-of-War. Prospects for US-European Cooperation. Festschrift in Honor of Helga Haftendorn*, ed. Ingo Peters (Münster: Lit-Verlag (forthcoming), 2006).

approaches towards Iran on both sides of the Atlantic, the growing policy coordination regarding this classical "backlash state" appears as an important anomaly in transatlantic relations after the end of the Cold War. This is why studying the case of Iran may help to determine factors that work in favor of greater transatlantic unity in the future.

2. Empirical Puzzle and Research Question

Europe and the United States have an historic track record of almost diametrically opposed approaches vis-à-vis Tehran.[11] For more than two decades, Washington emphasized the "rogue" aspects of Iran's behavior: pursuit of nuclear weapons, support for terrorism, opposition to the Middle East peace process as well as a poor human rights record.[12] This perception of the country led the U.S. to lobby its European allies to join Washington in isolating and confronting Iran for its 'bad behavior.' While most European countries shared American concerns, the EU continuously underlined the country's potential as a stabilizing regional power in the Middle East. Due to comparatively friendly bilateral affairs and an extensive economic involvement in Iran, this view was most ardently held in Germany.[13] Central to Berlin's perception of Iran was the assumption that the country's behavior could be moderated, so that it would incrementally play a more positive role in the Middle East.[14]

This fundamental strategic divide—Washington favoring a mix of containment and confrontation with Iran, European governments preferring dialogue and engagement—widened with the advent of the Bush administration in 2001. By labeling Iran part of an "Axis of Evil" in his State of the Union address in 2002, President Bush ratcheted up the pressure towards the Iranian regime and looked poised to provoke a serious transatlantic rift. Even more troublingly from a European point of view, the Bush administration seemed to embark on a policy of regime change towards Iran.[15] Members of the Bush cabinet, including the President, spoke out repeatedly in favor of democratic change and greater freedom in Iran. In November 2003 Bush made one of several only thinly veiled threats:

"In Iran, the demand for democracy is strong and broad [...]. The regime in Tehran must heed the

---

[11] As Peter Rudolf observed in 1997, "[n]owhere is the divergence of foreign policy strategies between the United States and Germany greater than in the case of Iran." Peter Rudolf and Geoffrey Kemp, "The Iranian Dilemma. Challenges for German and American Foreign Policy," (Washington, DC: AICGS, 1997), 1.

[12] Kenneth M. Pollack, *The Persian Puzzle. The Conflict between Iran and America* (New York: Random House, 2005) xxi. Additionally see: Henning Riecke, *The Most Ambitious Agenda. Amerikanische Diplomatie gegen die Entstehung neuer Kernwaffenstaaten und das Nukleare Nichtverbreitungsregime*, 2006, *Digitale Dissertation* (Freie Universität Berlin, 2002) 178-179.

[13] An excellent overview on the history of bilateral German-Iranian relations can be found in: Lane, "Germany's New Ostpolitik."

[14] For a good overview of the traditional differences between German and American perceptions of Iran see: Rudolf and Kemp, "The Iranian Dilemma."

[15] Reuel Marc Gerecht, *Regime Change in Iran?* American Enterprise Institute, 1 August 2002 [6 April 2006]; available from http://www.aei.org/publications/pubID.14201/pub_detail.asp.

democratic demands of the Iranian people, or lose its last claim to legitimacy.'"[16]

By questioning the domestic legitimacy of the Iranian regime, President Bush made the case that Iran could be denied its existential rights as a sovereign country.

Against the backdrop of the transatlantic disagreements over Iraq (2002/2003), this sort of rhetoric frightened many Europeans. The Bush administration's unilateral push for war with Baghdad demonstrated that Washington's doctrine of "preemptive warfare," as enshrined in the National Security Strategy of 2002, was of direct relevance to the conduct of U.S. foreign policy. Worse still, it seemed to remain a central guidepost for future challenges emanating from 'rogue states.'[17]

When Iran's nuclear program emerged as the most pressing international security issue in the shadows of the beginning Iraq War, Washington's belligerent rhetoric and unilateralist tendencies did not bode well for transatlantic cooperation on the challenge. As Germany, France and the UK started to engage Iran to prevent further nuclear proliferation in the summer of 2003, there was little hope in European capitals that the Bush administration would eventually opt to support their efforts.

Against the odds, America's approach towards Iran saw considerable changes in recent years which brought the Bush administration a lot closer to European policy preferences towards Iran.[18] The confrontational rhetoric of the President's "Axis of Evil" speech calmed down and the administration's foreign policy became, as the Economist put it, "so multilateral that Mr. Bush even seems willing to let France and Germany be involved in one of his main national security policies, namely stopping Iran from getting the bomb."[19]

It was in early 2005, when Washington adjusted its course for the first time by reaching out to its European allies: Departing from its traditionally confrontational path, the Bush administration seemingly suddenly allowed for greater transatlantic unity on one of the most challenging "rogue states." A more recent and more visible change—the Washington Post called it the perhaps "biggest foreign policy shift" of the Bush administration—occurred in May 2006.[20] Secretary of State Condoleezza Rice declared that Washington was prepared to join the multilateral negotiation

---

[16]   The White House, *President Bush Discusses Freedom in Iraq and Middle East Remarks by the President at the 20th Anniversary of the National Endowment for Democracy* 6 November 2003 [20 April 2006]; available from
http://www.whitehouse.gov/news/releases/2003/11/20031106-2.html.

[17]   The President of the United States of America, "The National Security Strategy of the United States of America," (Washington, D.C.: The White House, September 2002). The National Security Strategy essentially set out a doctrine of "preventive warfare," as opposed to "preemptive warfare." For clarification see: Karl-Heinz Kamp, "Von der Prävention zur Präemption? Die neue amerikanische Sicherheitsstrategie," *Internationale Politik*, no. 12/2002 (2002) 19-24.

[18]   For stylistic reasons—and in spite of slightly different meanings—the terminology "change," "adjustment," and "shift" of U.S. Iran policy will be used interchangeably throughout the following chapters.

[19]   Lexington, "Hard-line and soft-line in foreign policy," *The Economist* 23 October 2003.

[20]   Glenn Kessler, "Shift in U.S. Stance Shows Power of Seven-Letter Word," *Washington Post*, 1 June, 2006, A13.

process with Iran that Germany, France and the UK had initiated three years ago with the so called E3 process. She also announced that the U.S. would provide major incentives for Iran—a major sign of good-will and something which Washington had vehemently and consistently opposed prior to Rice's declaration.[21]

In this book I aim to analyze the underlying sources of these important and puzzling adjustments of U.S. Iran policy and the subsequent growth of transatlantic policy coordination. Inspired by relevant International Relations (IR) theory adapted to improve our understanding of U.S. foreign policy, the study seeks to devise an answer to the following guiding question:

Why has American Iran policy shifted towards supporting the European approach between 2003 and 2006?

Viewed in a larger context, the case of Iran serves as an *exemplar* for other "backlash states" and strategic security challenges which demand common transatlantic approaches in the future.

Drawing on neorealist and liberal IR approaches, the book arrives at the conclusion that Washington was unable to formulate an autonomous—i.e. unilateral—policy according to its original preferences of sanctioning and isolating Iran at the outset of the crisis in 2003. Faced with a lack of good military options and a rapid decline of political influence around the world after the controversial invasion of Iraq in 2003, the U.S. was forced to reconsider its approach towards Iran. During President Bush's first term in office (2000-2004), the dysfunctional character of the U.S. national security policy team prohibited changes in favor of European-led multilateral diplomacy. But personnel changes in the second administration allowed for (gradual) policy adjustments. However, the shifts in 2005 and 2006 can be best explained by a combination of three factors: First, America's freedom of action was considerably constrained due to a loss of political power in 2003 and 2004. Second, a streamlining process within President Bush's foreign policy staff after his re-election in November 2004 paved the way for a revised approach towards Iran. Third, the growing influence of Germany—especially after Angela Merkel was elected Federal Chancellor—and other European allies on the process of formulating Iran policy contributed to closer transatlantic policy coordination.

Before presenting the three theoretical perspectives that underpin my analysis and help to reach these conclusions, I shall describe the dependent variable—U.S. adjustments in Iran policy—in greater detail.

---

[21] Ibid.

3. The Dependent Variable: Adjustments of U.S. Iran Policy

This section provides additional empirical background that helps to understand the context of the adjustments of U.S. Iran policy between 2003 and 2006—the dependent variable—more adequately.[22] Because the challenge posed by Iran's suspicious nuclear activity gained momentum at the beginning of 2003 and transatlantic policy coordination reached a peak in at the end of May 2006, this book focuses on events between 2003 and May 2006.

During the summer of 2002, an Iranian dissident group helped to set off a chain reaction of international investigations, leading to the disclosure of Iran's clandestine nuclear activities. Caught red-handed, Tehran was forced to admit that it had secretly constructed a gas centrifuge plant in the vicinity of Natanz and a heavy-water production facility at Arak in defiance of its obligations to report these activities under the Nuclear Non-Proliferation Treaty (NPT).[23] Intelligence services and security experts on both sides of the Atlantic had long suspected that Iran was concealing some of its nuclear activities. But the new information dwarfed all customary expectations, both with regard to the scope and the progress of the program, and triggered the involvement of the International Atomic Energy Agency (IAEA). In February 2003, Mohamed ElBaradei, the IAEA's Secretary General, embarked on the first of many fact-finding missions inside Iran.

More importantly, Iran's secret nuclear activities demanded political reactions from Washington and European capitals where the possibility of a potentially nuclear-armed Iran (including the many implications of such a scenario) rang the alarm bells of decision-makers. In the summer of 2003, President Bush declared that the United States would not tolerate the construction of a nuclear weapon by Iran.[24] In the absence of formal diplomatic relations, which were cut off between the U.S. and Iran in 1979, and a trade embargo against the country, Washington looked poised revert to its traditionally confrontational stance by increasing pressure on its allies to sanction and further isolate the country. In fact, the Bush administration's inflammatory rhetoric towards Iran continued

---

[22]   For a good overview on different concepts about foreign policy change see: Monika Medick-Krakau, "Außenpolitischer Wandel: Diskussionsstand - Erklärungsansätze - Zwischenergebnisse," in *Außenpolitischer Wandel in theoretischer und vergleichender Perspektive: Die USA und die Bundesrepublik Deutschland*, ed. Monika Medick-Krakau (Baden-Baden: Nomos, 1999), 5-10. The term purely descriptive term "adjustment" is borrowed from Hermann. See: Charles F. Hermann, "Changing Course: When Governments Choose to Redirect Foreign Policy," *International Studies Quarterly* 34, no. 3 (1990) 3-21.

[23]   Pollack, *The Persian Puzzle* 361.

[24]   David E. Sanger, "Bush Says U.S. Will Not Tolerate Building of Nuclear Arms by Iran," *New York Times*, 19 June 2003, A1.

in 2003, and a number of administration officials spoke of Iran as the next target on President Bush's freedom agenda.[25]

During the summer of 2003, Germany, France and the UK—or "E3" as they later became known—started to negotiate a deal with Iran under which it could avoid a referral to the UN Security Council by the IAEA. Conceptually, European negotiations with Iran were building on the traditional conditional engagement approach that laid at the heart of virtually all official EU-Iranian relations of the 1990s, e.g. the European Union's "critical dialogue." The new European deal with Tehran stipulated that the country would allay international concerns about its nuclear weapons ambitions in exchange for a boost in economic relations and technological support for its civilian nuclear program.

The nature of this approach was directly at odds with Washington's preferences that demanded a quick involvement of the UN Security Council to punish Iran for its defiant behavior. Hence, the 'Tehran Declaration,' issued by the E3 and Iran in October 2003, was met with skepticism in Washington.[26] President Bush demanded greater and improved cooperation between Tehran and the IAEA, and many in his administration believed that the E3 had been too conciliatory during the negotiations.[27] On a trip to European capitals in November 2003, Secretary of State Colin Powell showed his dissatisfaction with a resolution drafted by the E3 that did not include the threat of sanctions in case of Iranian noncompliance with IAEA demands.[28] Adhering to its traditionally suspicious view about Iranian intentions, the United States accused Iran of deception and remained unimpressed by E3 negotiations. Washington stayed at the sidelines when European negotiations with Tehran continued in 2004 to conclude a final settlement of the nuclear crisis. As a Bush administration insider told the Washington Post in September 2004, Washington's Iran policy was aimed at coercing Tehran "using international pressure, to get them to rid themselves of their nuclear program."[29]

The first visible change of this position occurred in early 2005. After a successful re-election campaign, the Bush administration began to adjust its policy vis-à-vis Europe with direct implications for the prospects of a transatlantic approach towards Iran.[30] In February 2005, Washington surprisingly endorsed the European negotiation efforts and even agreed to offer

25   Gerecht, *Regime Change in Iran?*
26   The White House, *Remarks by the Press Secretary on Iran* 21 October 2003 [13 June 2006]; available from
      http://www.whitehouse.gov/news/releases/2003/10/20031021-15.html.
27   A. Rüesch, "USA für mehr Druck auf Iran im Atomstreit," *Neue Zürcher Zeitung*, 20 November 2003, 3.
28   Ibid.
29   Eric Schmitt, "Pentagon Office in Spying Case Was Focus of Iran Debate," *New York Times*, 2 September 2004, A17.
30   Guy Dinmore and Hubert Wetzel, "President faces hard sell over Iran policy," *Financial Times (London)*, 25 February 2005, 8.

limited incentives to induce a behavioral change of a still defiant Iran.[31] After a summit meeting with German Chancellor Gerhard Schröder, President Bush proudly declared that the United States and Europe were now "on the same page" with regard to Iran.[32] This policy change represented a first tactical but nevertheless substantial departure from the previous confrontational American position, that left no room for a *quid pro quo* compromise on Iran's nuclear program.

While Washington endorsed the E3-led negotiations, it still refrained from joining the engagement effort, something which European countries were hoping for. Meanwhile, Iran rejected a comprehensive offer from Germany, France and the UK in August 2005 remaining defiant of IAEA demands. Instead of resorting to its traditional confrontational policy towards Iran, Washington continued the commitment to multilateral diplomacy. Even after the election of the radical Iranian President Mahmoud Ahmadi-Nejad dampened the prospects of successful engagement with Tehran, the U.S. moved closer to the E3 position. On May 31, 2006 Condoleezza Rice assured Iran that Washington remained committed to a diplomatic solution of the crisis, that it was ready to join the E3 effort of multilateral negotiations, and that it would provide more inducements for Iranian compliance with IAEA demands. As Rice stated:

> "The benefits of this second path for the Iranian people would go beyond civil nuclear energy and could include progressively greater economic cooperation. The United States will actively support these benefits both publicly and privately. Furthermore, President Bush has consistently emphasized that the United States is committed to a diplomatic solution to the nuclear challenge posed by the Iranian regime.

> We are agreed with our European partners on the essential elements of a package containing both the benefits if Iran makes the right choice, and costs if it does not. [...]

> The United States is willing to exert strong leadership to give diplomacy its very best chance to succeed. Thus, to underscore our commitment to a diplomatic solution and to enhance the prospects for success, as soon as Iran fully and verifiably suspends its enrichment and reprocessing activities, the United States will come to the table with our EU-3 colleagues and meet with Iran's representatives."[33]

This statement contained at least three important messages marking the preliminary end of an evolutionary process in U.S. Iran policy. It reflected how far the Bush administration had adjusted

---

[31] Robin Wright, "Bush Weighs Offers to Iran; U.S. Might Join Effort to Halt Nuclear Program," *Washington Post*, 28 February 2005, A01. Bush also changed his stance on a plan from Russia that would supply Iran's Bushehr power plant with nuclear fuel—another indication of a more pragmatic and flexible approach. Cf. Steven R. Weisman, "U.S. Reviewing European Proposal for Iran," *New York Times*, 28 February 2005, A6.

[31] Sonni Efron, "Bush Softens Stance on Iran," *Los Angeles Times*, 12 March 2005, A1.

[32] William Branigin, "Bush, Schroeder Oppose Iran's Nuclear Ambitions," *Washington Post*, 23 February, 2005.

[33] Condoleezza Rice, *Press Conference on Iran* State Department, 31 May 2006 [1 June 2006]; available from http://www.state.gov/secretary/rm/2006/67103.htm.

its initial position on Iran since 2003.[34] The key features of the new approach were a new commitment to multilateralism and transatlantic policy coordination, a demonstrated commitment to a diplomatic solution as opposed to direct threats towards Tehran, and active support for the E3 engagement approach of offering real and tangible incentives to induce a change in Iranian behavior. Crucially, the active support for the E3 approach included Washington's willingness to enter a direct dialogue with Tehran within the framework of multilateral talks.

In sum, adjustments of U.S. policy laid the foundation for a growing degree of transatlantic policy coordination on Iran between 2003 and 2006. Washington began to officially endorse European-led negotiations in February 2005. In May 2006, the Bush administration announced its readiness to become part of the negotiation process itself.

---

[34] Mathias Rüb, "Washingtons weiter Weg in der Iran-Politik," *Frankfurter Allgemeine Zeitung*, 2 June 2006, 5.

4.   Theoretical Framework

How can we approach the empirical conundrum of adjusting U.S. Iran policy and greater transatlantic policy coordination from the perspective of IR theory? This section presents the theoretical framework of the book and generates specific research propositions with regard to potential explanatory variables. Drawing on the insights of mainstream IR theory as well as empirical observations, I will devise three general hypotheses which provide different *ex post* interpretations and explanations for the empirical puzzle. The selection of these theoretical perspectives follows the aim of developing complementary outlooks that may enhance our understanding of the case in an empirically relevant manner.

The combination of neorealist and liberal approaches serves this purpose particularly well. Neorealist foreign policy theory puts the primary emphasis on the constraints under which a state's foreign policy is formulated and implemented. It allows us to consider the "big picture" aspects of U.S. foreign policy in recent years. Additionally, two liberal approaches, which take into account the domestic dimension of U.S. foreign policy, serve as complementary bottom-up counterparts. The first liberal perspective (which I call Liberalism I) enables us to highlight the Bush administration's internal dynamics and their effects on Iran policy. The second liberal perspective (Liberalism II) allows us to draw attention to the transatlantic dimension by taking a closer look at how Germany—as part of the E3—has influenced Washington's stance on the issue.

It is important to note that the theory-derived hypotheses are not necessarily competitive with regard to their explanatory ambitions and individual scope. They present different angles from which the issue is looked at and they have distinct grasps with regard to independent variables. The three perspectives serve as different lenses that allow us to highlight specific aspects of the empirical puzzle. They produce different *ex post* narratives as to how we can explain and understand the adjustments of U.S. Iran policy and growing transatlantic policy coordination.

4.1.   Neorealist Foreign Policy Theory

Power-based perspectives constitute an obvious point of departure for explaining U.S. foreign policy.[35] Although neorealist approaches have been primarily concerned with theorizing on the level of the international system (therefore oftentimes called "structural realist"), they may well be adapted to enhance our understanding of a particular state's foreign policy.[36] Neorealists start from the assumption that the international system lacks a central governing authority and that its standard governing principle is therefore anarchy. States are the main relevant actors and constitute the international system. They are characterized as *units*, i.e. as unitary actors, whose actions are egotistical and instrumentally rational. The foreign policy of a state is chiefly informed by its capabilities- or power-based status within the international system, i.e. a state's own capabilities and its relative power vis-à-vis other states. As Stephen Krasner noted:

> "The behavior of individual states, regardless of their domestic political characteristics, is constrained by their own capabilities and the distribution of power in the system as a whole. The external environment will inevitably pressure states to move toward congruity between commitments and capabilities."[37]

Hence, a state's foreign policy is constrained by its absolute power as well as by its relative power. A state's absolute power can be understood as the availability of political, economic and military capabilities. A state's relative power describes the actual influence that is connected to that power, i.e. the ability of a state to assert its interests regarding other states. Due to the anarchical structure of the international system, which does not provide security for its *units*, states primarily strive to enhance their security status. Baumann, Rittberger and Wagner distinguish two forms of power politics which serve the purpose of enhancing state security: autonomy-seeking and influence-seeking foreign policy.[38] Autonomy-seeking foreign policy is aimed at increasing or preserving a

---

[35]   Neorealist IR theory as developed by Kenneth Waltz is chiefly based on Hans-Joachim Morgenthau's work. Arising in opposition to idealism, Morgenthau argued that politics is governed by rationality, that states are the most important actors in international affairs and that state's interests are defined 'in terms of power.' Hans-Joachim Morgenthau, *Politics Among Nations. The Struggle for Power and Peace* (New York: Alfred A. Knopf., 1948).

[36]   For an adaptation of neorealism as a theory of foreign policy see: Rainer Baumann, Volker Rittberger, and Wolfgang Wagner, "Neorealist foreign policy theory," in *German foreign policy since unification. Theories and Case Studies*, ed. Volker Rittberger (Manchester: Manchester University Press, 2001). Kenneth Waltz is widely regarded as the key proponent of neorealism: Kenneth N. Waltz, *Theory of International Politics* (Reading: Addison-Wesley, 1979). For a critical appraisal of Waltz and neorealism see: Robert O. Keohane, ed., *Neorealism and its Critics* (New York: Columbia University Press, 1986).

[37]   Stephen D. Krasner, "Power, Polarity, and the Challenge of Disintegration," in *America and Europe in an Era of Change*, ed. Helga Haftendorn and Christian Tuschoff (Boulder: Westview Press, 1993), 21. Cit in: Baumann, Rittberger, and Wagner, "Neorealist foreign policy theory," pp. 42.

[38]   Baumann, Rittberger, and Wagner, "Neorealist foreign policy theory," 45-58. The following paragraph draws on their main points on "influence-" and "autonomy-seeking" foreign policy.

state's level of independence vis-à-vis other states. Autonomy-seeking policies can be expected from states that are faced with a looming loss in independence of action. In this context, multilateral decision-making structures such as international institutions, can be seen as a key constraint on state's autonomy. There are different modes of state behavior that qualify as autonomy-seeking foreign policy:[39]

- non-compliance with, or withdrawal from, existing obligations resulting from bilateral or multilateral international agreements;

- the refusal to accept new obligations that are codified in bilateral or multilateral international agreements;

- the refusal to transfer national material resources to other states or international and supranational institutions; and

- the refusal to cooperate with other states whenever the degree or nature of cooperation threatens to limit a state's autonomy.

Additionally, autonomy-seeking foreign policy may aim at the formation of an alliance against a third state. As Baumann, Rittberger and Wagner note, "[a]t first glance, it may appear counter-intuitive that, in the case of alliances, cooperation is regarded as enhancing a state's autonomy."[40] Neorealism, however, allows for cooperation among alliance partners and a resulting minimal loss of autonomy, if it is aimed at prohibiting a third state from diminishing a state's autonomy to an even greater extent. According to Stephen Walt, the formation of alliances can be understood as balancing behavior against threatening powers.[41] Balancing behavior is more likely than alignment, and occurs when states form alliances with others against a prevailing threat, e.g. Iran. As Walt notes, instead of automatically balancing against or aligning with a superior power, states will consider and assess multiple factors to determine the nature of the impending threat prior to making alliance choices.[42] Threats are defined in terms of power—namely aggregate power, i.e. size of the population, industrial and military capabilities and technological prowess—but they also encompass geographic proximity, offensive capabilities and aggressive intentions.[43] Consequently, a

---

[39]   Adapted and augmented from: Ibid., 46.

[40]   Ibid.

[41]   Alliances are defined as "formal or informal relationship of security cooperation between two or more sovereign states." As Walt explains, "[t]his definition assumes some level of commitment and an exchange of benefits for both parties; severing the relationship or failing to honor the agreement would presumably cost something, even if it were compensated in other ways." Stephen M. Walt, *The Origins of Alliances* (Ithaca: Cornell University Press, 1987) 1.

[42]   By refining the relatively indeterminate concept of "balance of power" to a more testable "balance of threat" theory, Stephen Walt has sought to increase the predictability of state behavior by neorealist theory.

[43]   Stephen M. Walt, "Containing Rogues and Renegades: Coalition Strategies and Counterproliferation," in *The Coming Crisis. Nuclear Proliferation, U.S. Interests, and World Order*, ed. Victor A. Utgoff (Cambridge/London: MIT Press, 2000), Walt, *The Origins of Alliances*.

neorealist perspective must also take into account how Iran's power status and behavior might have influenced U.S. policy.

While balancing behavior, like all autonomy-seeking behavior, is aimed at reducing the impact of the international environment on a particular state's independence, influence-seeking foreign policy is aimed at impacting this very environment, i.e. other states, to shape it in ways favorable to a state's own interests. Influence-seeking policies are mainly conducted within international institutions but they may also occur in bi- or multilateral settings. As Baumann, Rittberger and Wagner state, the following policies can be categorized as influence-seeking:[44]

- an increase in voice opportunities in international organizations, bi- or multilateral frameworks, by increasing the state's own share in the intra-organizational resources (e.g. voting rights), or by increasing the commitment to the bi- or multilateral framework;
- preference for those multilateral institutions or frameworks that yield the most voice opportunities;
- securing voice opportunities regarding the policies of groups of states; and
- the establishment, maintenance or reinforcement of the dependence of weaker states (i.e. influence on these states).

Generally speaking, neorealist foreign policy theory expects states to seek more of both, autonomy and influence, the more power (i.e. opportunities for actually pursuing autonomy- and influence-seeking policies) they wield. As one version of neorealist thinking emphasizes, however, the "security pressures" on states can vary, and states will make their choices on whether to seek autonomy or influence based on the actual intensity of the threat they are faced with. In line with Walt's balance of threat theory, this variant of neorealism assumes that sheer power does not necessarily constitute a threat, but that many factors, such as geographic proximity and offensive intentions will be taken into consideration as well.

Drawing on the core tenet of neorealism—that state behavior is chiefly determined by its power position within the international system—Robert Kagan gave a widely-cited explanation of the muscular approach in U.S. foreign policy, following the terrorist attacks of 9/11 and of the more general differences between Europe and the United States with regard to foreign policy.[45] According to Kagan, Americans and Europeans inhabit two different planets when it comes to exercising military power and approaching the strategic, security-related challenges of the world. As Kagan has it, the U.S., living on planet Mars due to its powerful position, is acting as the world's fire

---

[44] The following points are an adapted and amended version from: Baumann, Rittberger, and Wagner, "Neorealist foreign policy theory," 47.

[45] Robert Kagan, "Power and Weakness," *Policy Review*, no. June & July (2002) 3-28.

brigade taking care of the most imminent security threats. European countries, according to their much less powerful position, concentrate on diplomatic means and the promotion of peaceful cooperation among states. According to Kagan, these different roles are not mainly determined by cultural factors, such as historical experience, but due to the imbalance of power resources between the U.S. and Europe. To substantiate this assertion, Kagan emphasizes that these roles have in fact changed over time, following changes in the distribution of capabilities.

> "When the United States was weak, it practiced the strategies of indirection, the strategies of weakness; now that the United States is powerful, it behaves as powerful nations do. When European great powers were strong, the believed in strength and martial greatness. Now, they see the world through the eyes of weaker powers. These very divergent points of view, weak versus strong, have naturally produced different strategies and judgements, differing assessments of threats and the proper means of addressing threats, and even different calculations of interests."[46]

The adjustments of U.S. Iran policy between 2003 and 2006 seem to contradict Kagan's assertion that American and European perspectives are differing on the "all-important question of power."[47] Instead of being unable to understand each other and to agree on matters of strategic importance, the United States and Europe seem to have diverged from Kagan's planetary straitjackets.[48]

Following Kagan's logic and neorealist foreign policy theory as outlined above, one would assume that the adjustments of U.S. Iran policy can be attributed to a loss of U.S. power between 2003 and 2006. According to neorealist expectations, this loss of power negatively affected Washington's ability to conduct an independent/autonomous Iran policy and forced it to rely on E3 diplomacy with Iran instead. In consequence, as some neorealists would point out, the U.S. had trouble to reconcile autonomy-seeking with influence-seeking foreign policy preferences. Generally speaking, neorealist foreign policy theory arrives at the following hypothesis to explain the adjustment in U.S. Iran policy between 2003 and 2006.

> As America's relative power position vis-à-vis other states diminished in recent years, U.S. foreign policy adjusted accordingly.

---

[46]   Ibid.
[47]   Ibid.
[48]   For thoughtful critiques of Kagan see: Elizabeth Pond, *Friendly Fire. The Near-Death of the Transatlantic Alliance* (Washington, D.C.: Brookings Institution Press, 2004), Szabo, *Parting Ways*. Kagan himself has interpreted the new transatlantic unity as a ploy of the Bush administration: Robert Kagan, "On Iran, Giving Futility Its Chance," *Washington Post*, 13 July 2006, A23.

4.2.   Liberal Foreign Policy Theory I

Liberal approaches to foreign policy concur that the driving forces in international relations are societal actors, determining a state's preferences and, thus, its foreign policy.[49] In other words, a state's foreign policy reflects the preferences of governments and societies in an aggregated form. Liberalism therefore regards the neorealist concept of states as unitary actors having stable national interests as ill-suited to explain foreign policy. According to Thomas Risse, liberal foreign policy perspectives agree on three core assumptions:[50]

1. The fundamental agents in international politics are not states but individuals acting in a social context—whether governments, domestic societies, or international institutions;

2. the interests and preferences of governments have to be analyzed as a result of domestic structures and coalition-building processes responding to social demands as well as external factors such as the material and social structure of the international system;

3. international institutions, that is "persistent and connected sets of rules (formal and informal) that prescribe behavioral roles, constrain activity, and shape expectations," form the social structure of international politics and present constraints as well as opportunities to state actors. [51]

As Corinna Freund and Volker Rittberger have emphasized, it is useful to develop an agency-based conceptual model to generate plausible liberal hypotheses that aim at explaining a state's foreign policy.[52] Such conceptual models, primarily seeking to explain U.S. governmental action, have been presented by Graham Allison and Philipp Zelikow. As Gert Krell and others have argued, Allison's and Zelikow's Models II and III—"Organizational Process" and "Governmental Politics"—can be seen as part of the liberal paradigm.[53] The core of these models can be summed up as follows. Instead of conceiving governmental action as the action of a unitary actor, Allison and Zelikow state that the decision maker of national policy is not "one calculating individual but is rather a

[49] See for example: Andrew Moravcsik, "Taking Preferences Seriously. A Liberal Theory of International Politics," *International Organization* 51, no. 4 (1997) 513-553, Thomas Risse-Kappen, *Cooperation Among Democracies. The European Influence on U.S. Foreign Policy* (Princeton: Princeton University Press, 1995).

[50] Risse-Kappen, *Cooperation Among Democracies. The European Influence on U.S. Foreign Policy* 25.

[51] Robert O. Keohane, *International Institutions and State Power* (Boulder: Westview, 1989) 3. Cit in: Risse-Kappen, *Cooperation Among Democracies. The European Influence on U.S. Foreign Policy* 25.

[52] Baumann, Rittberger, and Wagner, "Neorealist foreign policy theory," 72-100.

[53] Gert Krell, *Weltbilder und Weltunordnung. Einführung in die Theorie der Internationalen Beziehungen*, 3rd ed. (Baden-Baden: Nomos, 2004) 219-227, Ursula Lehmkuhl, *Theorien Internationaler Politik. Einführung und Texte*, 3rd ed. (München: R. Oldenbourg Verlag, 2001) 135-141.

conglomerate of large organizations and political actors."[54] By opening up what neorealist foreign policy theory conceives as a "black box," the authors suddenly look at a far more complicated picture. Following from this trivial but important observation, changes in foreign policy can then also occur when the structure of the international system and the distribution of capabilities among states remains stable. The prime agent of change is then to be identified by looking at the make-up of a government, for it is the interplay between a range of actors within a government that produces political decisions. Allison's Model II, "Organizational Process," assumes that governments consist of different organizational structures and perceives problems through organizational sensors. Governmental behavior can therefore be understood as an output of large organizations, functioning according to standard patterns of behavior that are partially coordinated by a unified group of leaders. Accordingly, foreign policy challenges—such as Iran—are broken down according to organizational lines and dealt with in an only partially coordinated fashion. Rather than weighing all possible courses of action, the group of leaders chooses the type of action that adequately addresses the issue. In doing so, organizations, for example the White House, the Department of Defense or the Department of State, follow their respective standard operating procedures when dealing with policy challenges. Model II leads the analyst to clarify what organizations the government consists of and which organizations traditionally act on the problem under analysis.

Going even further, Allison's and Zelikow's Model III, "Governmental Politics," regards government action as the result of a bargaining game between powerful individuals inside the government. Instead of perceiving governments as being made up of a unified group of leaders "Governmental Politics" conceives this group as consisting of individual players that determine policy in a central, competitive game. Confronted with a foreign policy challenge, these individuals usually disagree on its resolution. Government behavior can then be understood as political resultant. *Political* in the sense that the activity from which decisions emerge is best characterized as bargaining along regularized channels among individual players, e.g. in the Bush administration. *Resultant* in the sense that what happens is not chosen as a specific solution to a particular problem but rather results from compromise, conflict, and confusion of officials with diverse interests and unequal influence. Individuals become players in the national security policy game by occupying a position that is connected to the major channels for producing action on national security issues. In the U.S. government, players include *Chiefs* (e.g. the President, the Secretary of State, the Secretary of Defense, the Vice President, the National Security Advisor), *Staffers* (the immediate staff of each

---

54   Graham T. Allison and Philip D. Zelikow, *Essence of Decision. Explaining the Cuban Missile Crisis*, 2nd ed. (New York: Longman, 1999) 3.

chief), *Indians* (political appointees within each of the departments and agencies) and *Ad Hoc Players* (such as Congress, the press, pressure groups, etc.). The position of a player defines obligations as well as limitations as to what he/she must or may do. Each individual player enters the game with distinct personal characteristics, perceptions and interests. Central to a player's impact on governmental behavior is his/her power, i.e. effective influence on government decisions and actions. This influence is primarily constituted of bargaining advantages (resulting from positional power, resources, information, etc.).

Allison's and Zelikow's Model II and III focus on identifying which institutions and individual players are centrally involved in formulating Iran policy. It leads us to ask what preferences these players and organizations stand for, and how they have tried to influence policy. In adapting Allison's models to explain adjustments in U.S. Iran policy, we must document how changes in the make-up of the government have affected or caused these adjustments. Central changes of the make-up of the Bush administration's foreign policy team occurred after President Bush's re-election in November 2004. The following hypothesis captures the core of the Liberal Foreign Policy Theory I perspective.

As the set of dominant players in charge of formulating U.S. foreign policy changed after President Bush's re-election in November 2004, American foreign policy adjusted accordingly.

4.3.   Liberal Foreign Policy Theory II

There is another theoretical perspective on the adjustments of U.S. Iran policy which can be derived from the liberal paradigm. Liberal foreign policy theory does not only look at the domestic dimension of foreign policy, it also stresses the impact of transgovernmental relations that affect state interests and preferences. [55] Liberal theorists have developed the concept of 'policy interdependence' which provides the crucial link between varying state behavior and changing state preferences. According to Andrew Moravcsik, policy interdependence can be understood as the set of costs and benefits for foreign societies that arise when a given society seeks to realize its own

---

[55]   Cf. Moravcsik, "Taking Preferences Seriously. A Liberal Theory of International Politics."

national preferences.[56] Liberal approaches posit that this pattern of interdependence among state preferences influences and constrains state behavior.

This liberal perspective merits consideration due to the empirical observations made in the introductory chapter. U.S. Iran policy appears to have changed more decisively than European Iran policy between 2003 and 2006, and Washington has been amenable to European policy preferences since 2005. If we assume, as Helen Milner has argued, that the internal organization of states follows polyarchic rather than hierarchic designs, domestic and international affairs are inextricably linked.[57] This perspective allows us to analyze the influence of other states on U.S. foreign policy on a less abstract level. From Liberal Foreign Policy Theory II point of view, we may conceptualize Washington's European allies as a separate entity (or player), which, despite not being a formal member of the Bush administration, may have impacted Washington's decision making on Iran. In adapting Allison's and Zelikow's models, one can conceptualize states like Germany as an *Ad Hoc Player* in the game of defining U.S. Iran policy.

Additionally, based on the Kantian notion of "democratic peace," some liberal arguments posit that democracies form "pluralistic security communities" of shared values.[58] The interaction between democratically elected governments is embedded in commonly held notions of democratic values, while also reflecting domestic decision-making norms. According to this perspective, smaller states like Germany, can influence the making of American foreign policy by altering Washington's estimates about how it should respond to international challenges such as Iran.[59] Furthermore, the transatlantic community of democracies allows for transgovernmental and transnational coalition-building processes to advance certain policies. Consultation norms between allies are the primary enabling feature that allows governments to influence each other on various issues. As Risse explains, "[t]he obligation to regularly consult each other can then be regarded as the functional equivalent to domestic norms regulating the publicity of the political process, its constitutionality, and the equality of the participants."[60] As conceptualized here, Liberal Foreign Policy Theory II focuses on how Washington's European allies may have affected U.S. Iran policy. Because this book focuses on the impact of Germany, Liberal Foreign Policy Theory II stipulates the following hypothesis.

---

[56] Andrew Moravcsik, "Liberal Theories of International Relations," *Unpublished Working Paper, Princeton University* (2006).

[57] Helen V. Milner, *Interests, Institutions, and Information. Domestic Politics and International Relations* (Princeton: Princeton University Press, 1997).

[58] Risse-Kappen, *Cooperation Among Democracies. The European Influence on U.S. Foreign Policy* 26.

[59] Ibid. 34.

[60] Ibid. 35.

As the set of dominant players in charge of formulating U.S. foreign policy changed, (new) transatlantic channels of communication emerged, allowing for greater influence of Germany. American policy adjusted accordingly.

5.   Methodology, Sourcing and Structure

In sum, the three theoretical approaches put forward different causes (or independent variables) for the changes observed in U.S. Iran policy. They also produce different narratives as to why U.S. policy has seen adjustments between 2003 and 2006. In short, neorealist foreign policy theory puts emphasis on changes in relative U.S. power. Liberal foreign policy theory highlights changes of policy preferences inside the Bush administration, in the first case due to internal re-arrangements or change of the dominant players (Liberal Foreign Policy Theory I) and in the second, due to greater influence of Germany, an important European U.S. ally (Liberal Foreign Policy Theory II). In order to operationalize the insights of the three theoretical approaches, we need to devise a methodological approach which sets out indicators that support the plausibility of the hypotheses.

According to the neorealist perspective, an analysis of U.S. Iran policy must provide an answer to the question whether Washington's power position in relation to Iran and other countries has seen changes between 2003 and 2006. If so, we should look for instances where this decrease of military, economic or political power has forced the U.S. to make adjustments in favor of European Iran policy. Neorealist foreign policy can solve the empirical puzzle, when it can be conclusively argued that the United States compromised its traditional autonomy-seeking policy in favor of increasing influence on the E3 to affect Iranian behavior. It should be possible to argue that U.S. adjustments occurred due to the fact that Washington's relative power resources did not allowed for continued autonomy-seeking policy.

In order to analyze the validity and plausibility of this explanation, I will first draw on quantitative and qualitative data to describe and evaluate the state of American power. By employing a process-tracing method, I will then look for instances in which a causal relationship between a loss of U.S. power and its policy vis-à-vis Iran can be assumed. Empirical data for this part of the analysis will mainly be derived from daily newspaper sources. To enhance the explanatory power of neorealism, it will be important to look for causal mechanisms that allow us to link Washington's power status and its foreign policy preferences.

Liberal foreign policy theory considers domestic structure as the foremost *determinant* of U.S. foreign policy. Liberalism I focuses on the dominant organizations and individual actors within the Bush administration impacting the formulating of foreign policy. To analyze the dependent variable from this viewpoint, we must first identify and describe the dominant actors and organizations that were centrally involved in the process of formulating policy on Iran and outline their respective preferences. This may be facilitated by highlighting the roles of individual players in reaching critical political decisions on Iran and by looking at how public statements on Iran policy reflect different positions within the Bush administration.[61] In doing so, we should be able to track changes with regard to the involvement of actors and organizations determining U.S. foreign policy and corresponding policy changes. For the first George W. Bush administration we can draw on a limited number of inside accounts detailing the individual preferences of the main players involved in formulating U.S. foreign policy. Among others, investigative journalist Bob Woodward has been able to document the internal deliberations of the Bush administration on the Iraq War and beyond in his books "Bush at War," "Plan of Attack" and, more recently, "State of Denial."[62] A number of other inside accounts can also be taken into consideration.[63] Since many of the internal deliberations on Iran have yet to be reviewed and analyzed in a comprehensive fashion, the bulk of empirical data has to be extracted from newspaper sources and public statements from the Bush administration. It will be important to trace how decision making on Iran within the "group of leaders" has changed in accordance with changes in the make-up of the Bush cabinet.

Liberal Foreign Policy Theory II attributes the adjustments of U.S. Iran policy indirectly to a growing influence of Germany, one of America's European allies. Influence on the process of formulating U.S. foreign policy is difficult to measure, and there are multiple ways in which Berlin could have affected decision making in the United States. A necessary precondition for impacting U.S. foreign policy preferences is that influential players inside the administration are amenable to European policy preferences in the first place.[64] In this context, it will be important to come to terms with the logic of the E3 approach towards Iran and develop an understanding of European preferences on the issue. On the basis of this analysis, we can then trace how Germany, acting in concert with the E3, has tried to promote a change in U.S. Iran policy. As in the other cases, in order not to neglect possible causal mechanisms not hypothesized before, I will employ a process tracing method. Drawing on Risse's propositions of when to expect smaller states to significantly impact the leader of a democratic alliance, the following indicators shall be employed. Allied influence on U.S. Iran policy can be deemed significant if U.S. decision makers consider, endorse or incorporate policy proposals on Iran originally developed by its European allies and if transnational

---

[61] The endeavor is clearly dependent on the availability of relevant and satisfying empirical data.

[62] Bob Woodward, *Bush at War* (New York: Simon & Schuster, 2002), Bob Woodward, *Plan of Attack* (New York: Simon & Schuster, 2004), Bob Woodward, *State of Denial: Bush at War, Part III* (New York: Simon & Schuster, 2006).

[63] For example: Seymour M. Hersh, *Fact: The Coming Wars. What the Pentagon can now do in secret* The New Yorker, 24 January 2005 [31 May 2005 available from http://www.newyorker.com/fact/content/?050124fa_fact, Seymour M. Hersh, *Fact: The Iran Plans. Would President Bush go to war to stop Tehran from getting the bomb?* The New Yorker, 17 April 2006 [31 May 2006 available from http://www.newyorker.com/fact/content/articles/060417fa_fact, David J. Rothkopf, *Running the World. The Inside Story of the National Security Council and the Architects of American Power* (New York: PublicAffairs, 2005).

[64] We can draw on the analytical insights from the Liberal Foreign Policy Theory I perspective to verify that this precondition has been met at the time where allied influence is analyzed.

and transgovernmental coalition-building characterizes interallied interactions.[65] To facilitate the task of demonstrating European influence on formulating U.S. policy vis-à-vis Iran, I focus on Germany, an E3 country that stands out for a number of reasons. Berlin's Iran policy builds on an exceptionally solid bilateral relationship with the country. Germany serves as Tehran's prime export partner and has been the most resolute supporter of a negotiated settlement of the nuclear crisis in a multilateral setting.[66] It has also repeatedly urged the United States to engage more actively in this process, and balked publicly at the prospect of possible military action against Iran.[67] Rather than focusing on France or the United Kingdom, tracking Germany's influence on U.S. foreign policy is therefore particularly relevant.[68]

In the following chapter (B.), I will systematically examine U.S. Iran policy between 2003 and 2006 from the viewpoint of the three theoretical perspectives. The final chapter (C.) provides a summary of my findings and draws conclusions relevant to transatlantic coordination of policies towards Iran.

---

[65]   Risse-Kappen, *Cooperation Among Democracies. The European Influence on U.S. Foreign Policy* 25.

[66]   John C. Hulsman and James Philips, "Forging a common transatlantic approach to the Iranian nuclear problem," *Heritage Foundation Backgrounder*, no. 1837 (23 March 2005).

[67]   Johannes Leithäuser, "Eine oft vorgetragene Frage. Berlin hat Washington zu Verhandlungen mit Teheran aufgefordert," *Frankfurter Allgemeine Zeitung*, 2 June 2006, 5.

[68]   This is even more true if one considers German-American relations in a broader context and with regard to the recent crisis over the Iraq War. For a comprehensive overview, see: Szabo, *Parting Ways*.

B.   Three Perspectives on U.S. Iran Policy

1.   Neorealism: Power on the Wane

As alluded to in the previous section, any neorealist analysis of a country's foreign policy must start
with an evaluation its the power position in the international system and the corresponding realm of
its freedom of action.

Neorealists have developed the following narrative about the emergence of the structure of the
international system as we know it today. For a start, from the Treaty of Westphalia in 1648 until
the Second World War the system has been marked by multipolarity—with many different rising
and falling powers. From 1945 until the collapse of the Soviet Union in the early 1990s, the
structure can be best described as bipolar—with the two superpowers facing each other. Following
the end of bipolarity, the United States emerged as the sole superpower.[69] In an attempt to describe
America's relationships with the rest of the world, political commentators frequently refer to this
common place perception by using the analogy of the United States as the "New Roman Empire."[70]
Shortly before the invasion of Iraq in 2003, some American politicians argued that the United States
has in fact become a "super-duper power" due to its enormous military supremacy.[71] Even scholars,
who tend to be skeptical about imperialistic foreign policy designs, agree with the notion that the
structure of the international system can be characterized as "unipolar"—the United States being
the all dominant pole.[72] As Nicholas Gvosdev observed in 2006, "[d]uring the last several years it
seems as if every major book or article on American grand strategy contains the observation that

---

[69]   Cf. Philip H. Gordon, "The Transatlantic Alliance and the International System," in *Conflict and Cooperation in Transatlantic Relations*, ed. Daniel Hamilton, *Transatlantic Books* (Washington, D.C.: SAIS Center for Transatlantic Relations, 2004), 75.

[70]   For a critical voice see: Michael Lind, *Is America the New Roman Empire?* The Globalist, 19 June 2002 [12 June 2006]; available from http://www.theglobalist.com/DBWeb/StoryId.aspx?StoryId=2526.

[71]   The somewhat ironic sounding phrase "super-duper power" was coined by former Republican House Majority Leader Tom DeLay. FOXNews.com, *House Majority Whip Backs Iraq Action* 22 August 2002 [13 July 2006]; available from www.foxnews.com/printer_friendly_story/0,3566,60998,00.html. For an influential argument defending the notion of almost limitless U.S. power see: Kagan, "Power and Weakness." Additionally, see the bulk of Charles Krauthammer's commentary in the Washington Post between 1992 and 2006.

[72]   See for example: G. John Ikenberry, "America's Imperial Ambition," *Foreign Affairs* 82, no. September/October (2002), G. John Ikenberry, ed., *America Unrivaled. The Future of the Balance of Power, Cornell Studies in Security Affairs* (Ithaca: Cornell University Press, 2002).

the United States is more powerful than any international actor since the Roman Empire was at its zenith."[73]

Neorealist foreign policy theory leads us to expect that the United States has suffered a remarkable loss of this global power projection capability between 2003 and 2006. It also leads us to expect that its adjusted Iran policy can be directly attributed to this loss of power. However, since there is no commonly accepted standard for defining the features of powerful states, we must first come to terms with the task of assessing the U.S. "power" position. A comprehensive analysis of U.S. power must take into consideration its military, economic and political aspects as well as their development between 2003 and 2006.[74]

1.1. Decline of U.S. Military, Economic and Political Power?

If we perceive the world solely in military terms, it can surely be described as "unipolar." In 2003 the Bush administration proposed a defense budget of US$ 379.9 billion, roughly ten times what Britain or France are spending in absolute terms, or twice as much as the other NATO member states combined.[75] After the terrorist attacks of 9/11, America's defense budget saw the biggest increase since the end of the Cold War.[76] This trend continued and accelerated until 2006. Measured in terms of its defense budget, U.S. military power has seen rapid increases rather than losses in recent years. Contrary to neorealist expectations, this is similarly true for U.S. economic power. America's economic performance—as measured by gross domestic product (GDP) growth—has been stable during the years of 2003 to 2006. Although the Iraq War in 2003 and the subsequent occupation of the country required major shifts in financial resources to the military, U.S. GDP continued to grow solidly in 2004 and 2005. While hurricane Katrina caused far-reaching damage in the U.S. Gulf Coast region in August 2005, it had a small impact on general GDP growth. The same is true for the rapid increase of oil prices since 2004. While higher costs for oil threatened inflation and unemployment in the United States as elsewhere, the American economy continued to grow throughout mid-2006.[77]

---

[73] Nicholas Gvosdev, *Crisis of American Power: Layne, Tucker, Hendrickson* The Washington Realist, 1 August 2006 [12 September 2006]; available from http://washingtonrealist.blogspot.com/2006/08/crisis-of-american-power-layne-tucker.html.

[74] Following neorealist theory and the primacy attributed to "relative power," Iran's power position will also have to analyzed as a reference.

[75] Vernon Loeb, "As Military Spending Booms, Budget Debate Looms," *Washington Post*, 16 February 2003, A19.

[76] Ibid.

[77] CIA, *The World Factbook: United States* Central Intelligence Agency, 2006 [12 September 2006]; available from https://www.cia.gov/cia/publications/factbook/geos/us.html#Econ.

If U.S. military power (as measured by defense spending) and economic power (as measured by GDP growth) has remained stable in recent years, in which other areas can we identify a possible decline of U.S. power? An answer to this question leads away from a purely quantitative evaluation of U.S. power to an assessment defined by qualitative standards.[78]

What comes to mind are the far-reaching consequences of the U.S.-led Iraq War—America's most demanding mission since the Vietnam War—and its wider implications for America's ability to make use of its military, economic and political power around the world. Although President Bush essentially declared U.S. victory on May 1, 2003, almost 150.000 U.S. troops remain stationed in Iraq until today.[79] Despite its military might, the U.S. failed to suppress a growing insurgency and to stabilize the country after main fighting was declared over. The lasting occupation of Iraq put a visible drag on U.S. military capabilities: The U.S. Army in particular suffered in the aftermath of Operation Iraqi Freedom in recent years.[80] Consequently, the Iraq War and its development until 2006 has reduced U.S. military capabilities, especially the possibility of a full-scale ground invasion in other countries.[81] The Iraq War also focused much of the Bush administration's attention and financial resources on suppressing the insurgency and reconstructing the country, leaving less attention for the Iranian nuclear issue.[82] As Kenneth Pollack put it:

> "Iraq was soaking up the lion's share of America's military forces, diplomatic capital, and economic assistance funds. There was very little of any of these items left for another major problem such as Iran."[83]

Following the Iraq War, military options to stop the Iranian nuclear program—which looked more suitable before the invasion of 2003—lost much of their appeal. In the fall of 2004, a war gaming exercise showed that the U.S. military was too strained by its commitments in Iraq to mount a full-scale invasion of the country, and that less comprehensive military options, i.e. air strikes on Iranian nuclear facilities, would only increase the determination of Iran to build nuclear weapons.[84] Furthermore, Iran's capabilities to retaliate against a U.S.-led military campaign were judged to be

---

[78]   In their evaluation of Germany's improved power position following the 1990 re-unification, Baumann, Rittberger and Wagner rely solely on quantitative assessments. Baumann, Rittberger, and Wagner, "Neorealist foreign policy theory."

[79]   CNN.com, *Commander in Chief lands on USS Lincoln* 2 May 2003 [12 February 2006]; available from http://www.cnn.com/2003/ALLPOLITICS/05/01/bush.carrier.landing/.

[80]   For a comprehensive assessment of the effects of the Iraq War on U.S. armed forces see: Lynn E. Davis et al., *Streched Thin: Army Forces for sustained operations* (Santa Monica: RAND Corp., 2005).

[81]   Cf. James Phillips, John C. Hulsman, and James Jay Carafano, "Countering Iran's Nuclear Challenge," in *Backgrounder* (Washington, DC: The Heritage Foundation, December 14, 2005).

[82]   On a monthly basis, the Bush administration spent an average of about $6.4 billion for Operation Iraqi Freedom. For a detailed analysis of the costs related to "war on terror" operations see: Amy Belasco, "The Cost of Iraq, Afghanistan, and Other Global War on Terror Operations Since 9/11," (Congressional Research Service, 2006).

[83]   Pollack, *The Persian Puzzle* 368-369.

[84]   James Fallows, "Will Iran be Next? Soldiers, Spies, and Diplomats Conduct a Classic Pentagon Wargame-With Sobering Results," *The Atlantic Monthly* December 2004.

manifold.[85] As Sam Gardiner, a retired U.S. Air Force Colonel, concluded: "You have no military solution for the issues of Iran. And you have to make diplomacy work."[86] In this context, it is also important to note that the United States lacked other unilateral options to put pressure on Iran, such as further economic isolation or other forms of sanctioning behavior.[87]

Although difficult to measure, the military invasion of Iraq has also directly and indirectly contributed to a decline in American political power, or what Joseph Nye has termed "soft power." According to Nye, soft power is the "ability to attract others by the legitimacy of U.S. policies and the values that underlie them." [88] U.S. soft power declined as Washington squandered the international sympathy which followed the attacks of 9/11 by focusing on "unipolarity, hegemony, sovereignty and unilateralism."[89] As Charles Grant argued, the decline of American soft power in recent years has been astounding.[90] Although not necessarily representative for elite views of the United States, the annual survey *Transatlantic Trends* by the German Marshall Fund has captured how America's image in the world declined in recent years.[91] As Andrew Kohut and Bruce Stokes pointed out, U.S. reputation suffered almost universally since the invasion of Iraq.[92] Joseph Cirincione pointedly captured the apparent decline of U.S. respect and influence around the world when he stated:

> "Never in American history has there been a six years period that has witnessed such a precipitous decline in American power and prestige. Never have we been so isolated in the world. Never have we been so hated. Never have we been so weakened. And it's our own doing. No enemy did this to us."[93]

---

[85] Ibid. See also: Paul Rogers, "Iran: Consequences of a War," in *Briefing Paper* (Oxford: Oxford Research Group, February 2006).

[86] Quoted in: Fallows, "Will Iran be Next?."

[87] Since President Clinton signed two executive orders that prohibited investment in Iran by American companies in 1995 and the U.S. Congress passed the Iran-Libya Sanctions Act (ILSA), which extended sanctions to include foreign companies making investments in Iran in excess of $20 million, Washington has essentially exhausted all available economic "sticks" against Iran.

[88] Joseph S. Nye, "The Decline of America's Soft Power," *Foreign Affairs* 84, no. May/June (2004).

[89] Joseph S. Nye, *The Paradox of American Power: Why the World's Only Superpower Cannot Go it Alone* (Oxford: Oxford University Press, 2002).

[90] Charles Grant, "The Decline of American Power," *CER Bulletin*, no. Issue 29 (April/May 2003).

[91] Transatlantic Trends is an annual public opinion survey examining American and European attitudes towards the transatlantic relationship and other international issues. Recent reports can be viewed via the website: http://www.transatlantictrends.org.

[92] Cf. Andrew Kohut and Bruce Stokes, *America Against the World: How We Are Different And Why We Are Disliked* (New York: Times Books, 2006).

[93] Joseph Cirincione in a debate at the CATO institute: CATO Institute, *Ethical Realism: A Vision for America's Role in the World, A Cato Institute Book Forum featuring the authors Anatol Lieven, New America Foundation; John Hulsman, German Council on Foreign Relations; with comments by Lawrence Kaplan, The New Republic; and Joseph Cirincione, Center for American Progress.* 10 October 2006 [13 October 2006]; available from http://www.cato.org/event.php?eventid=3227.

1.2.   An Emboldened and More Powerful Iran

While Washington was deprived of the ability to mount a ground invasion of Iran and dramatically lost political influence around the world, Tehran's strength as a regional power grew visibly between 2003 and 2006.

Iran's power position must be analyzed in the context of its geostrategic location. Drawing on a vast territory, a large population (roughly three times that of Iraq) and rich oil and gas reserves Iran perceives itself as a potential regional hegemon. [94] Tehran's relative power position increased dramatically when Iran's prime regional enemies—the Taliban in Afghanistan and Saddam Hussein in Iraq—were removed from power.[95] The rise of oil and gas prices in recent years has contributed to Iran's economic well-being and empowered it to act more boldly on the international stage. Tehran's political calculations were far more cautious before the Iraq War when oil prices were around $25 per barrel. As Karim Sadjapour observed, the Iraq War and the steep rise of crude oil prices have "essentially given new life to the regime in Tehran."[96] Military action against Iran could easily set the barrel price to $100 or even $120 which would have highly negative ramifications for the U.S. and world economy.[97] Against this backdrop, Iran's growing confidence and more assertive stance on the nuclear issue in recent years comes as no surprise. Seen from a neorealist perspective, Mahmoud Ahmadi-Nejad's forceful new leadership style and his uncompromising stance on the nuclear program are merely an outgrowth of Iran's improved power position within the international system.[98]

1.3.   Analysis of U.S. Iran Policy (2003-2004)

To sum up, from a neorealist perspective—taking into account "soft power" in addition to the traditional neorealist components of a country's capabilities—we can point out three different

---

[94]   Kamran Bokhari, *The Nuclear Deadlines and a Strengthening Iran* 22 August 2006 [24 August 2006]; available from http://www.stratfor.com/.

[95]   Ilan Berman, *Tehran Rising: Iran's Challenge to the United States* (Lanham: Rowman & Littlefield, 2006). For a more nuanced view see: Geoffrey Kemp, *Iran and Iraq: The Shia Connection, Soft Power, and the Nuclear Factor* United States Institute of Peace, November 2005 [13 March 2006]; available from http://www.usip.org/pubs/specialreports/sr156.html.

[96]   Karim Sadjapour quoted in: Scott Peterson, *Why Iran sees no rush for a nuke deal* Christian Science Monitor, 2006 [7 September 2006]; available from http://www.csmonitor.com/2006/0907/p06s02-wome.html.

[97]   For a good summary of the constraints on U.S. options for dealing with Iran see: Josef Joffe, *Oil, Sweat and Fears. While containing and deterring Iran, there is time for talks* Atlantic Times, May 2006 [10 June 2006]; available from http://www.atlantic-times.com/archive_detail.php?recordID=492.

[98]   Cf. Ibid, Peterson, *Why Iran sees no rush for a nuke deal.*

factors, which have impacted U.S. Iran policy between 2003 and 2006:

- limited U.S. military options vis-à-vis Iran, primarily due to the continued large-scale U.S. military presence in post-war Iraq;
- decreasing U.S. political (or "soft") power, due to wide-spread international opposition to the Iraq War and the war on terrorism more generally; and

increasing Iranian regional influence (due to the overthrow of the regimes in Afghanistan and Iraq, as well as increased revenues from crude oil sales). Keeping these factors in mind, let us now turn to the analysis of U.S. Iran policy from the perspective of neorealist foreign policy theory.

In 2003, the United States was set on pursuing an autonomy-seeking policy vis-à-vis Iran. Shortly after the beginning of the Iraq War in March, Washington seemed to be very confident in its military power as it tried to threaten Iran with military action to counter its apparent involvement in Iraq. In April, Washington complained that the *Badr corps*—the military forces of the Supreme Council for Islamic Revolution in Iraq (SCIRI)—that was trained, equipped and directed by Iran, had entered Iraq from Iranian territory.[99] The U.S. considered this behavior a "hostile act" and announced that the Iranian regime would be held to account.[100] From a neorealist perspective, this reaction can be seen as flowing from a position of strength after the relatively easy military victory in Iraq. Washington perceived Iran's meddling in Iraq as a direct threat to the security of its military forces and its geopolitical foothold in the Middle East region. This temporary U.S. self-perception of strength also played out with regard to the nuclear issue and merged with America's longstanding view of Iran as a "rogue state." Washington was chiefly interested in censuring Iran for hiding the non-civilian parts of its nuclear program from the IAEA.

In accordance with neorealist expectations, Washington sought to transfer the Iran file from an international organization in which it held less "voice opportunities" (the IAEA's board of governors), to an international organization where it had more influence to shape international action on Iran (the UN Security Council, where the U.S. is holding a veto-wielding seat). Accordingly, during the fall of 2003, Washington attempted to enlist IAEA member states to support a strong resolution against Iran which would provide the basis for a referral to the United Nations.

In accordance to this strategy, the Bush administration's disapproved of the deal which Germany, France and the UK brokered with Iran during the summer of 2003. Washington stated that the

---

[99] Toby Harnden, "US accuses Syria and Iran of 'hostile acts'," *Telegraph*, 29 March 2003.

[100] Ibid. The Badr Corps' main military goal was to defeat the Mujahedeen-e-Khalq (MEK)—an anti-Iranian militia group—who allied itself with Baghdad after the Islamic revolution in 1979. See: Globalsecurity.org, *Badr Corps* [17 May 2006]; available from http://www.globalsecurity.org/military/world/para/badr.htm.

signing of the NPT's Additional Protocol—as promoted the E3 in the "Tehran Declaration" of October 2003—would not be enough to assure Iran's compliance with its obligations under the Non-Proliferation Treaty.[101] Unlike the E3, Washington was unwilling to participate in a *quid pro quo* deal based on direct negotiations with Iran.[102] In November 2003, U.S. officials continued to lobby the members of the IAEA board of governors—especially Germany, France, and the UK—for a resolution that would threaten Iran's referral to the UN Security Council.[103] As a neorealist perspective helps to show, however, Washington was forced to drop its request for a tough approach at the insistence of European powers and the IAEA's director general at a board of governors meeting in late November.[104] The European powers took the diplomatic lead on Iran, while the U.S. was dealing with the issue from a position of weakness. Washington realized that its influence to garner support for a tough approach would not succeed due to a lack of influence at the IAEA.[105]

Neorealist foreign policy theory categorizes state behavior that shows a preference for multilateral institutions or frameworks that yield to the most "voice opportunities," as influence-seeking policy. This influence-seeking approach continued to be the core of U.S. Iran policy in 2004. President Bush's statement that "Iran will be dealt with, starting through the United Nations," reflected Washington's interest to gain greater influence on the issue by asserting American leadership.[106]

As Iran started to become more assertive itself (by violating the terms of the Tehran Declaration in early 2004), the United States also sought to balance Tehran by means of autonomy-seeking policies.[107] Faced with a lack of unilateral military or economic options, gaining autonomy vis-à-vis Iran required the formation of an international coalition by attracting the diplomatic support from other countries for U.S. preferences, most notably from Washington's European allies at the IAEA. As the neorealist perspective highlights, Iran's growing assertiveness helped to further this goal. Tehran's initial cooperative stance with the E3—Mohamed ElBaradei spoke of a "sea change" in

---

[101]   U.S. Department of State, *Interview by The Washington Post* 1 October 2003 [13 June 2006]; available from http://www.state.gov/secretary/former/powell/remarks/2003/25139.htm. See also: The White House, *Roundtable Interview of the President by the Press Pool, Aboard Air Force One, En Route Canberra, Australia* 22 October 2003 [4 May 2006]; available from http://www.whitehouse.gov/news/releases/2003/10/20031022-7.html.

[102]   Rüesch, "USA für mehr Druck auf Iran im Atomstreit."

[103]   Ibid.

[104]   Steven R. Weisman, "U.S. acquiesces to allies on new Iran resolution; Nuclear issue will not be referred to UN," *New York Times*, 26 November 2003, 3.

[105]   Ibid.

[106]   Mike Allen, "Iran 'Will Be Dealt With,' Bush says; Bid to Start at UN, President Says," *Washington Post*, 22 April 2004, A06.

[107]   This form of power politics primarily serves the purpose of increasing or preserving a state's level of independence vis-à-vis other states, in this case U.S. independence vis-à-vis Iran.

Iran's cooperation since October 2003—changed in 2004.[108] When IAEA inspectors discovered designs for advanced centrifuges (P-2) to be used for uranium enrichment, the 'Tehran Declaration' seemed to be falling apart.[109] In light of the new findings, which indicated a much more complex and secretive Iranian nuclear program than previously assumed, American officials at the IAEA began to work more intensely on assembling an international coalition.[110] U.S. Iran policy now aimed at using "bilateral and multilateral pressure, [to] secure international consensus against Iran's pursuit of enrichment and reprocessing capabilities."[111]

As Washington tried to assemble an international coalition, it continued to pressure the IAEA board of governors to report Iran to the UN Security Council. [112] This dual track approach continued when American diplomats sought the support of other countries for a tough U.S.-sponsored resolution at IAEA's board of governors meeting in September 2004.[113] Washington became impatient with the slow progress at the IAEA, and tried to rally support by highlighting the threat posed by Iran and pointing to failures of the European engagement approach. As National Security Advisor Condoleezza Rice stated before a critical meeting in Vienna: "The Iranians have been trouble for a very long time." [...] "This regime has to be isolated in its bad behavior, not quote-unquote, engaged."[114] The statement was a direct rebuff off the European approach of directly talking to the Iranians.

Despite this tough rhetoric, however, Washington had to face the reality of its limited influence at the IAEA. The U.S. draft resolution, which again pushed for UN Security Council action on Iran, did not attract much support from the IAEA's 35-member board. Washington sweetened the resolution, by promising that the UN's involvement was only sought to support continued IAEA inspections in Iran. [115] European IAEA members, however, rebuffed Washington again and overruled "key language sought by the United States and disagreed with [...] most details of the

---

[108] The Economist, *Iran, Libya and nukes* 13 March 2004 [12 May 2006]; available from
http://www.economist.com/world/africa/displaystory.cfm?story_id=E1_NVDPDGN.

[109] Ian Traynor, "Europe's nuclear deal with Iran faces collapse," *The Guardian (London)*, 14 February 2004, 16. See also: Dafna Linzer, "Iran Says It Will Renew Nuclear Efforts," *Washington Post*, 25 June 2004, A01. At the same time, it became apparent that Iran had been cooperating with the "nuclear Wal-Mart" network of A.Q. Khan. Peter Brooks, *Nuclear Wal-Mart* The Heritage Foundation, February 2004 [17 May 2006]; available from http://www.heritage.org/Press/Commentary/ed020904a.cfm.

[110] Nikolas Busse, "Beratungen über Iran-Resolution; Widerstand gegen europäisch-amerikanischen Entwurf," *Frankfurter Allgemeine Zeitung*, 12 March 2004, 8.

[111] U.S. Department of State, *The Bush Administration's Nonproliferation Policy: Successes and Future Challenges. John R. Bolton, Under Secretary for Arms Control and International Security, Testimony Before the House International Relations Committee* 30 March 2004 [3 June 2006]; available from http://www.state.gov/t/us/rm/31029.htm.

[112] Ibid. See also: Dafna Linzer, "No Progress in Nuclear Talks with Iran; U.N. Discussions Likely After European Effort, Powell Says," *Washington Post*, 30 July 2004, A14.

[113] Dafna Linzer, "Iran Negotiates Deal to Curtail Nuclear Work; U.S. Sees Offer as Bid to Stall Sanctions," *Washington Post*, 8 September 2004, A14.

[114] Guy Dinmore and Gareth Smyth, "Support grows for UN showdown with Iran over nuclear programme," *Financial Times (London)*, 5 August 2004, 9.

[115] Linzer, "Iran Negotiates Deal to Curtail Nuclear Work; U.S. Sees Offer as Bid to Stall Sanctions."

final resolution."[116]

From a neorealist point of view, due to the limits of U.S. sway at the IAEA, the E3 again succeeded in taking the diplomatic lead on Iran. On November 14, 2004 Germany, France and the UK concluded the "Paris Agreement" with Tehran, which clarified the rather vague terms of the "Tehran Declaration" from 2003. Following this second European-Iranian agreement, the IAEA was again able to report positive assessments of Iranian cooperation with inspectors, a development that directly undermined U.S. efforts to seek punitive measures.[117] On November 28, the IAEA board of governors passed a resolution sponsored by Germany, France and the UK that welcomed Iran's decision to continue the suspension of all enrichment related and reprocessing activities.[118] It also included an endorsement of the "Paris Agreement." Previous to the passing of this resolution, Washington again failed to promote its own views on Iran at the IAEA.[119]

1.4.   Analysis of U.S. Iran Policy (2005-2006)

Viewed through the lens of neorealist foreign policy theory, the events at the IAEA in 2003 and 2004 seem to have directly triggered the adjustments of U.S. Iran policy in 2005 and 2006. The finite nature of U.S. political influence (or "soft power") in Vienna forced Washington to take more conciliatory stance on Europe's efforts to engage Iran, to make its influence-seeking policy work, and build up an international coalition to confront Tehran.

After his re-election in November 2004, President Bush indicated that he intended to reach out across the Atlantic and work with European nations to defuse the nuclear crisis.[120] The new Secretary of State, Condoleezza Rice, also sought to alleviate European fears of U.S. plans to tackle the Iranian nuclear issue militarily. As neorealists would point out, Rice took into account the obvious constraints on U.S. military power (at least partly due to U.S. military commitments in Iraq)

---

[116] Dafna Linzer, "Allies at IAEA Meeting Reject U.S. Stand on Iran; Draft Asks for Suspension of Nuclear Work," *Washington Post*, 18 September 2004, A22. See also: Steven R. Weisman, "Allies Resist U.S. Efforts to Pressure Iran on Arms," *New York Times*, 9 September 2004, A13.

[117] Dafna Linzer, "U.N. Finds No Nuclear Bomb Program in Iran; Agency Report and Tehran's Deal With Europe Undercut Thougher U.S. Stance," *Washington Post*, 16 November 2004, A18.

[118] The U.S. had failed to generate support for the insertion of a so-called "automatism clause" which would have allowed for a quick referral of Iran to the UN Security Council in case of non-compliance. Dafna Linzer, "Nuclear Agency Praises Iran; IAEA Supports Arms Pact, Won't Seek Sanctions," *Washington Post*, 30 November 2004, A01.

[119] The U.S. had failed to generate support for the insertion of a so-called "automatism clause" which would have allowed for a quick referral of Iran to the UN Security Council in case of non-compliance. Ibid.

[120] The White House, *State of the Union Address by the President* 2 February 2005 [8 June 2006]; available from http://www.whitehouse.gov/news/releases/2005/02/20050202-11.html.

by stating that Washington had "no intentions to attack Iran."[121]

On a more profound level, however, the U.S. started to accept the reality of its diminished political influence in Europe after the Iraq War. Washington realized that it would have to change its attitude with regard to the European negotiation process to counter the notion "that Europe was mediating between the United States and Iran."[122] While Washington was not giving up on seeking both influence and autonomy with regard to Iran, its tactics began to change. President Bush's trip to Europe in February 2005 was designed to increase U.S. sway in Europe, while at the same time laying the groundwork for an international coalition to confront Iran.[123] After the Mainz Summit with German Chancellor Gerhard Schröder on February 23, 2005 Bush declared that the United States and Europe were now "on the same page" regarding Iran. He also promised to consider a full endorsement of the E3 process and provide limited incentives to Tehran.[124] As neorealists would point out, the endorsement of the negotiation process served the purpose of preparing the formation of an anti-Iranian alliance in support of tougher actions under Washington's leadership in the future. Granting full support to the European engagement effort was not uniquely intended to increase U.S. influence by countering the notion that Washington was staying at the sidelines of the conflict and handing the Europeans "more cards to play in their negotiations with the Iranians."[125] If the new round of diplomacy would fail, the more conciliatory stance would also convince European powers to consider other measures against Iran, starting with the long-sought referral to the UN Security Council.[126]

In accordance with neorealist expectations, the surprise election of the radical Iranian President Ahmadi-Nejad in June 2005 increased the sense of urgency to coordinate Iran policy with the Europeans in Washington.[127] This view was underlined by Iran's uncooperative stance vis-a-vie the E3. Tehran confidently dismissed the European proposal to halt its suspicious nuclear activities in exchange for wide-ranging economic and political incentives and announced its decision to resume

---

[121] Steven R. Weisman and Judy Dempsey, "Rice works to bolster ties with Europe; She tries to assuage fears U.S. has any plans to attack Iran," *International Herald Tribune*, 5 February 2005, 1, Robin Wright, "Rice Says U.S. Won't Join Europe in Iran Nuclear Talks," *Washington Post*, 3 February 2005, A10.

[122] Condoleezza Rice, "Rice optimistic about Bush's bold agenda in his second term, partial transcript of Secretary of State Condoleezza Rice's interview with editors and reporters," *Washington Times*, 12 March 2005, A07.

[123] For example, Bush reiterated that while military options remained "on the table," Washington was not getting ready to attack Iran in the near future. Michael A. Fletcher and Keith B. Richburg, "Bush Tries to Allay E.U. Worry Over Iran; Notion of U.S. Attack 'Is Simply Ridiculous'," *Washington Post*, 23 February 2005, A01.

[124] Dinmore and Wetzel, "President faces hard sell over Iran policy."

[125] Efron, "Bush Softens Stance on Iran."

[126] Wright, "Bush Weighs Offers to Iran; U.S. Might Join Effort to Halt Nuclear Program." Bush also changed his stance on a plan from Russia that would supply Iran's Bushehr power plant with nuclear fuel—another indication of a more pragmatic and flexible approach. Cf. Weisman, "U.S. Reviewing European Proposal for Iran."

[127] Robin Wright, "U.S. and Europe Gird for Hard Line From Iran's President," *Washington Post*, 26 June 2005, A17.

uranium conversion at Isfahan in August 2005.[128]

Meanwhile, President Bush reaffirmed his commitment to a diplomatic solution and kept the door open for further rounds of negotiations between the Europeans and Iran.[129] In an effort to pursue its autonomy-seeking strategy, Washington lobbied Russia, India, and China as well as countries from the non-aligned movement (NAM) that were holding seats on the IAEA's board of governors, to support the referral of Iran to the UN Security Council.[130] But despite Washington's support for a European-drafted resolution censuring Iran, it was unable to reach a unanimous decision.[131]

Confronted with slow progress at the IAEA, Washington showed more flexibility with regard to exploring other options. Ahead of the critical IAEA board of governors meeting on November 24, 2005 the U.S. endorsed a proposal from Russia that would allow Iran to continue uranium conversion on its own soil while uranium enrichment activities would be conducted on Russian territory.[132] As neorealists point out, this new flexibility aimed at increasing Washington's leverage by convincing other countries that the U.S. had left no diplomatic option untried and was genuinely committed to the search for a diplomatic solution.[133] Following its two-track approach, Washington also concentrated on persuading Russia and China to agree on a timeframe for UN Security Council referral and specific punitive actions against Iran.[134] As Tehran became more openly aggressive—its new President had made threatening statements vis-à-vis Israel and showed no intentions to cooperate with the international community—an agreement with these two veto-wielding Security Council members had to be found not only for the referral itself but also with regard to subsequent UN-mandated action.

Between fall 2005 and early 2006, Washington showed considerable diplomatic flexibility to reach a consensus at the IAEA that allowed it to finally achieve the long-desired involvement of the UN Security Council.[135] At the critical IAEA meeting on February 4, 2006 the U.S. ambassador stated that it had been "[a] very important part of the board meeting [...] that the European Union, the

128 Dafna Linzer, "Iran Resumes Uranium Work, Ignores Warning," *Washington Post*, 9 August 2005, A10.
129 Dafna Linzer, "Bush Cautiously Optimistic as Iran Offers to Negotiate," *Washington Post*, 10 August 2005, A11.
130 Steven R. Weisman, "Wider U.S. Net Seek Allies Against Iran's Nuclear Plan," *New York Times*, 10 September 2005, A3.
131 Dafna Linzer and Colum Lynch, "U.S. Agenda on Iran Lacking Key Support," *Washington Post*, 16 September 2005, A26. See also: Mark Landler, "Nuclear Agency Votes to Report Iran to U.N. Security Council for Treaty Violation," *New York Times*, 25 September 2005, 6.
132 Dafna Linzer, "U.S. Backs Russian Plan To Resolve Iran Crisis," *Washington Post*, 19 November 2005, A16, Steven R. Weisman, "U.S. and Europe delay bid to refer Iran to UN," *International Herald Tribune*, 24 November 2005, 6.
133 Steven R. Weisman and David E. Sanger, "U.S. and Britain Try a New Track on Iran," *New York Times*, 4 December 2005, 14.
134 Steven R. Weisman, "U.S. and Allies Court Russia and China to Help Curb Iran," *New York Times*, 7 January 2006, A5. Also: Robin Wright, "U.S., France Warn Iran On Nuclear Program," *Washington Post*, 15 October 2005, A11.
135 Elaine Sciolino and Steven R. Weisman, "U.S. Compromises on Wording of Iran Nuclear Resolution," *New York Times*, 4 February 2006, A6.

United States, Russia and China stood together."[136]

As neorealists would point out, a combination of factors led to this "success" of U.S. Iran policy. First, Washington gained political influence at the IAEA and in its international diplomatic efforts more generally by showing a greater willingness to compromise. Second, Iran's overly confident and dismissive attitude vis-à-vis the IAEA and the E3 as well as the aggressive rhetoric of its new President towards Israel facilitated the coalition-building process to counter the "prevailing" Iranian threat.[137]

As the United States soon realized in early 2006, Russia and China would not "accept significant sanctions over the coming months, certainly not without further efforts to bring the Iranians around."[138] To get Russian and Chinese support for a chapter VII UN Security Council resolution (that would lay the foundations for U.S.-sought sanctions), the United States needed to further compromise. On March 30, after the UN Security Council agreed on a presidential statement that gave Iran 30 days to show goodwill by suspending its uranium enrichment activities, Condoleezza Rice met with the three European powers, Russia and China to discuss further actions.[139] The meeting concluded without any substantial agreement on how to proceed and the international coalition that Washington had worked to assemble, was at risk of falling apart.[140] Russia and China remained opposed to any form of sanctions against Iran.[141] Lacking viable military options and the capability for unilaterally imposed sanctions, the United States was forced to compromise again.

Seen from a neorealist perspective, the announcement of Washington's readiness to enter the multilateral negotiation process with Iran in May 2006 appears as a logical next step to keep the international coalition against Iran together. Similarly to the adjustments of early 2005, the shift in 2006 appears to be designed to provide the basis for tougher international action, e.g. UN-mandated sanctions, if Iran refuses to cooperate. As the Bush administration put it, the new policy forced Iran to choose between a "positive" and a "negative" path.[142]

---

[136] John Ward Anderson and Glenn Kessler, "U.N. Nuclear Agency Reports Iran to Security Council," *Washington Post*, 4 February 2006.

[137] Jim Hoagland, "Iran's Gift: New Unity in the West," *Washington Post*, 23 February 2006, A19.

[138] Times Online, *Leaked letter in full: UK diplomat outlines Iran strategy* 22 March 2006 [23 March 2006]; available from http://www.timesonline.co.uk/article/0,,2-2098203,00.html.

[139] Glenn Kessler, "Iran Warned, but Russia, China Dissent on Action," *Washington Post*, 31 March 2006, A16, Steven R. Weisman, "U.S. Accepts Draft on Iran that Omits Use of Force," *New York Times*, 31 May 2006, A10.

[140] Glenn Kessler, "Rice Key to Reversal on Iran; Expected Failure of International Effort Led to U.S. Turnaround," *Washington Post*, 4 June 2006, A17.

[141] Kessler, "Iran Warned, but Russia, China Dissent on Action."

[142] Rice, *Press Conference on Iran*.

1.5.   Summary

The neorealist perspective highlights that Washington's limited influence following the Iraq War forced the United States to rethink its position on Iran and adapt its policy accordingly. The security situation in Iraq required the U.S. to maintain high troop levels in the country and critically limited U.S. confrontational military options with Iran. Lacking international support for a more confrontational policy as desired at the outset of the nuclear crisis, the United States was bound to regain influence among the member states of the IAEA's board of governors by becoming more actively engaged in the diplomatic process with Iran. By means of influence-seeking policy Washington continuously sought to transfer the nuclear issue to the UN Security Council where its position as a veto-wielding member would allow it to exert greater control over the diplomatic process. With comprehensive unilateral economic sanctions against Iran already in place, the pursuit of a multilateral diplomatic strategy was a necessary prerequisite to further punish Iran.

At the same time, some factors worked in favor of Washington's desire to rally the international community against the country. Exploiting the fact that Washington was bogged down in Iraq, Tehran's threatening and uncompromising behavior—especially after the election of President Ahmadi-Nejad and the refusal of the E3 offer in August 2005—worked in favor of America's goal of involving the UN Security Council. The application of any form of UN-mandated sanctions, however, remained dependent on further international support, especially from Russia and China.[143] By means of autonomy-seeking policy Washington sought to assemble an international coalition that would hold together and confront Iran in the future. U.S. policy adjustments from May 2006 took into account that Washington would only be able to garner critical international support for tougher action by demonstrating its commitment to a diplomatic solution. According to the neorealist perspective, Washington's Iran policy balanced between the influence-seeking and autonomy-seeking impulses, the main driving forces of any state's foreign policy.

---

[143]   Kessler, "Rice Key to Reversal on Iran."

2.   Liberalism I: The Two Bush Administrations

The neorealist analysis highlights the prime constraints under which Washington's Iran policy was forced to operate between 2003 and 2006. As it points out, multilateral diplomacy remained the only viable path for U.S. policy. Neorealists have a hard time, however, understanding and explaining the finer print of American foreign policy. As Michael Rubin—a former Defense Department official—stated, the constraints on Washington, which neorealists readily attach great importance to, may have mattered differently than expected.

> "They [the Iranians] believe we're bogged down in Iraq. They may believe we're stymied in the
> UN by the Russians and Chinese. They may believe oil prices are too high for action. But the
> administration is deadly serious. Any military action would likely involve the air force and the
> navy, not the troops in Iraq. And while everyone recognizes the problems of any military action,
> there is a real belief that the consequences of Iran going nuclear would be worse."[144]

From the perspective of liberal foreign policy theory, the United States lacks a monolithic national interest. Rather than following the neorealist "billiard ball" model, the Bush administration is made up of different organizations and individual players with distinct interests, preferences, and impact on the formulation of U.S. foreign policy.

Allison's and Zelikow's Model II—Organizational Process—purports that U.S. policy towards Iran, like all U.S. foreign policy, is broken down according to organizational responsibilities. Different organizations inside the administration are dealing with policy issues according to pre-established repertoires of action. With regard to Iran, the Pentagon and the Department of State emerge as two organizations with key responsibilities on the formulation of U.S. policy. The State Department was chiefly responsible for the diplomatic efforts on the issue, while the Pentagon—as the organization responsible for the conduct of the Iraq War—perceived Iran mainly in terms of its military missions. Although difficult to measure unequivocally, both organizations have seen varying influence on the formulation of U.S. foreign policy between 2003 and 2006. The Pentagon's influence on U.S. foreign policy is closely connected with the Iraq War. In 2003, the Pentagon was arguably the prime organization determining the course as well as the conduct of U.S. foreign policy.[145] As Zbigniew Brzezinski stated regarding the Pentagon's role in shaping U.S. foreign policy in 2003:

---

[144]   Cit in: Marc Perelman, *U.S. Officials Are Mulling Iran Strikes, Experts Say* The Forward, 7 April 2006 [9 May 2006]; available from http://www.forward.com/articles/7616.

[145]   Karen DeYoung and Glenn Kessler, "Foreign Policy: After Iraq, U.S. Debates The Next Steps," *Washington Post*, 13 April 2003, A01.

"The fact is that in the Defense Department you have a cluster of people ... who have a strategic viewpoint that's strongly held and well-refined, and you don't have its equivalent in the State Department. [...] The State Department doesn't like the fact that the Defense Department takes the lead strategically, but it hasn't really formulated some alternative concept of how American foreign policy should be conducted. And that is weakness."[146]

In addition to leading the Iraq War, the Department of Defense was also in charge of the reconstruction efforts in the country until this task was re-assigned to the Department of State by President Bush in December 2005.[147] The Pentagon and the State Department were largely unable to coordinate their foreign policy efforts and perceived each other as rivaling organizations.[148]

Allison's and Zelikow's Model III—Governmental Politics—allows us to look at the different interests involved in formulating Iran policy by determining patterns of behavior that reach across organizational lines. In order to draw on the insights of Governmental Politics, we need to identify the dominant players having a hand in forging U.S. policy towards Iran.

Institutionally, President George W. Bush occupied the position of the most powerful player. As President, he determined the main course of U.S. foreign policy. With regard to the more specific designs, however, the President was not quite as involved. As White House observers have stated, the individual personalities around the President mattered more than usual during the first Bush administration because the President tolerated and even encouraged continuous clashes in his cabinet in regard to the shaping of foreign policy.[149] During the first term of his presidency, Bush's leadership style contributed and fueled internal disputes between leading members of his cabinet on foreign policy issues, including the conclusion of a coherent approach towards Iran.[150] As Kenneth Pollack noted, understanding the internal divisions between "hawks" and "doves" within the Bush administration is critical to explaining U.S. Iran policy.

"Some of the administration's hawks wanted to take a much more aggressive posture on Iranian nuclear activities [...]. Indeed, some wanted to try to mount an effort to overthrow the Iranian government via covert action or even launch military strikes against Iranian facilities. The doves in the administration wanted to try to solve the problem through diplomacy, which mostly meant

---

[146] Cit in: Ibid.

[147] Caroline Daniel and Guy Dinmore, *Pentagon loses responsibility for rebuilding Iraq* 15 December 2005 [12 June 2006]; available from http://www.ft.com/cms/s/4f826e9e-6d0f-11da-90c2-0000779e2340.html.

[148] As Bob Woodward remarked with regard to the interagency coordination process: "The fighting between the State and Defense departments was so bad that interagency meetings were at times little more than shouting matches." Bob Woodward, "Should He Stay? The biggest question mark was Secretary of Defense Donald H. Rumsfeld," *Washington Post*, 2 October 2006, A01.

[149] James Mann, *Rise of the Vulcans. The History of Bush's War Cabinet* (New York: Viking Penguin, 2004), David E. Sanger, "Who'd Be In, Who'd Be Out," *New York Times*, 17 October 2004, Woodward, *Plan of Attack*.

[150] Oftentimes, Bush reserved his final decision on internally contentious issues until the very last moment while his cabinet members were competing for his support. See: DeYoung and Kessler, "Foreign Policy: After Iraq, U.S. Debates The Next Steps."

assisting the European effort."[151]

Direct access to and a trustful relationship with the President was the *conditio since qua non* to influence policy on Iran. As Liberalism I points out, changes within the Bush administration, especially changes of personnel, were responsible for policy adjustments regarding Iran. Since significant changes in the make-up of the Bush administration's foreign policy team only followed after the presidential elections in November 2004, we must come to an understanding of the different *modi operandi* of the two Bush cabinets involved.

2.1.   Main Players in the First Bush Administration

Let us first take a look at the different policy preferences and the respective influence of the most important individual players (on the level of *Chiefs*, *Staffers* and *Indians*) of the first Bush administration. At the center of most internal disputes about Iran policy – on the level of the *Chiefs* – were Vice President Dick Cheney, Secretary of Defense Donald Rumsfeld and Secretary of State Colin Powell.[152] A long-time Bush confidant, Vice President Cheney was probably the most influential personality during the first Bush administration.[153] Cheney helped install some of his former associates to senior-level positions, including Rumsfeld, Paul Wolfowitz as Deputy Secretary of Defense, and I. Lewis Libby as his chief of staff.[154] Cheney assembled an influential group of national security experts in the Vice Presidents Office for the first time in U.S. history.[155] His influence on foreign policy was crucially connected with his main ally and friend in the cabinet Donald Rumsfeld. At the Pentagon, Rumsfeld also built a "kitchen cabinet" of special assistants and consultants within the Office of the Secretary of Defense that "grew into a fortress of old friends and retired military officers."[156] Along with others in the civilian leadership of the Pentagon, such as Undersecretary for Policy Douglas Feith (who himself led a "mini-State Department inside the Pentagon") and John Bolton at the State Department, the group around Cheney and Rumsfeld was generally on the record for a confrontational policy towards Iran.[157] Publicly or privately, most

---

[151] Pollack, *The Persian Puzzle* 368-369.

[152] DeYoung and Kessler, "Foreign Policy: After Iraq, U.S. Debates The Next Steps."

[153] Glenn Kessler, "Impact From the Shadows. Cheney Wields Power With Few Fingerprints," *Washington Post*, 5 October 2004, A01, Ted Koppel, *Cheney Wields Unprecedented V.P. Power. On Iraq and Elsewhere, Many Say Cheney Wields New Vice-Presidential Clout* ABC News, 29 November 2003 [12 May 2006]; available from http://abcnews.go.com/Nightline/story?id=129012.

[154] Rothkopf, *Running the World* 390-392.

[155] Kessler, "Impact From the Shadows. Cheney Wields Power With Few Fingerprints."

[156] Woodward, "Should He Stay?."

[157] Lexington, *United States Foreign Policy: The Shadow Men* The Economist, 24 April 2003 [12 June 2006]; available from http://www.economist.com/world/na/displayStory.cfm?story_id=1731327, James Risen and David Johnston, "Spy Case Renews Debate Over Pro-Israel Lobby's Ties to Conservatives at Pentagon," *New York Times*, 4 September 2004, 10.

of them had spoken out in favor of fomenting a revolution inside Iran in order to replace the Islamic regime.[158] As prominent neoconservatives within the Bush administration, Wolfowitz, Libby, Feith and Bolton perceived the Iraq War as part of a larger project of reforming the entire Middle East including Iran.[159] In their view, however, this democratization effort would not always necessitate the use of military force.[160]

This first group of administration officials was united by its overarching desire to replace the Iranian regime. Proponents of the "regime change" approach generally advocate the active support of and the arming of regime opponents inside and outside Iran, threats of military force, and covert operations against the Iranian regime. Regime change advocates often share the belief that removing the Iranian regime would solve the manifold troubles in the Middle East. This "regime change as a panacea" view is aptly summarized by Rob Sohani.

> "A secular, democratic, pro-American Iran would mean peace in the Persian Gulf. It would mean stability in Afghanistan. It would mean stability in Iraq. It would be an end to Iran's nuclear program. It would immediately put an end to terrorism, and it would add weight to, in a positive way to the Arab-Israeli peace process. A democratic Iran [...] is a better Iran as opposed to an Islamic Iran that we are trying to engage."[161]

While President Bush was clearly sympathetic to the overarching goal of encouraging democratic reform in the Middle East, he did not speak out in favor of a regime change approach towards Iran.[162]

The second camp of Bush administration "doves" held an openly critical view of the goal of "regime change" in Iran. Secretary of State Colin Powell, his *Staffers* and close friends Deputy Secretary of State Richard Armitage and Chief of Staff Lawrence Wilkerson, as well as *Indians* at the Near East Bureau of the State Department were opposed to this policy on the grounds that it seemed unattainable at an "acceptable price."[163] In an internationalist fashion, Powell and his associates were convinced that the U.S. would be well advised to work with its allies in Europe,

[158] Lexington, *United States Foreign Policy: The Shadow Men,* Risen and Johnston, "Spy Case Renews Debate Over Pro-Israel Lobby's Ties to Conservatives at Pentagon."

[159] Phil McCombs, "This Fire This Time; To Some Scholars, Iraq's Just Part of Something Bigger," *Washington Post,* 13 April 2003, F01. Wolfowitz, Libby, Feith and Bolton are prominents neoconservatives. Cf. Christian Science Monitor, *Neoconservatives and their blueprint for US power: Key figures* CSM, [12 June 2006]; available from http://www.csmonitor.com/specials/neocon/index.html.

[160] McCombs, "This Fire This Time; To Some Scholars, Iraq's Just Part of Something Bigger." Wolfowitz, Libby, Feith and Bolton are prominents neoconservatives. Cf. Christian Science Monitor, *Neoconservatives and their blueprint for US power: Key figures.*

[161] Rob Sohani in: PBS News Hour, *Threat From Tehran?* 27 May 2003 [8 May 2006]; available from http://www.pbs.org/newshour/bb/middle_east/jan-june03/iran_5-27.html#.

[162] Glenn Kessler and Peter Slevin, "Rice Fails to Repair Rifts, Officials Say; Cabinet Rivalries Complicate Her Role," *Washington Post,* 12 October 2003, A01. The White House, *President Discusses the Future of Iraq, Speech before the American Enterprise Institute* 26 February 2003 [13 June 2006]; available from http://www.whitehouse.gov/news/releases/2003/02/20030226-11.html.

[163] Barton Gellman and Dafna Linzer, "Unprecedented Peril Forces Tough Calls. President Faces a Multi-Front Battle Against Threats, Known, Unknown," *Washington Post,* 26 October 2004, A01.

Russia and China to prevent Iran from acquiring a nuclear weapon.[164] Although this approach involved increasing diplomatic pressure on Tehran, it was also open to trying to engage the Iranian regime, at least selectively.[165] Conceptually similar to the European form of engagement, senior State Department officials argued that the provision of rewards or incentives could shift the cost-benefit-analysis inside the Iranian regime and induce a change of behavior with regard to the central issues of concern.[166] Inside the State Department, Undersecretary of State for Arms Control John Bolton was vehemently opposed to any form of engagement.[167] While nominally reporting to the Secretary of State, Bolton's views on Iran were much closer to the confrontational approaches espoused by the Pentagon and the Vice President's office.[168] Because Bolton was actively pursuing a much tougher approach than his superiors (for example at the IAEA), he repeatedly clashed with Powell and Armitage on Iran and other national security related issues.[169] As the leading U.S. envoy on nonproliferation, Bolton aggressively pressed for punitive actions by the UN Security Council against Iran during the first Bush administration.[170]

National Security Advisor Condoleezza Rice was caught in the midst of the battle between "hawks" and "doves" on formulating a coherent approach towards Iran. A close confidante of President Bush, Rice was influential but oftentimes unable to mediate between the different positions of Rumsfeld, Cheney and Bolton on the one hand and Powell and the State Department on the other. [171] Among Rice's National Security Council (NSC) staffers were advocates of a confrontational approach towards Iran—like Eliot Abrams—as well as proponents of conditional engagement, like Robert Blackwill, and non-ideological pragmatists like Meghan O'Sullivan.[172] Rice herself appeared to be divided about the problem, willing to try a diplomatic approach before

---

164   Mike Allen, "Powell Announced his Resignation; Secretary of State Clashed With Cheney and Rumsfeld; Rice to Succeed Him," *Washington Post*, 16 November 2004, A01, U.S. Department of State, *Interview by The Washington Post.*

165   In a testimony before the Senate International Relations Committee in 2003 Armitage struck a demonstratively conciliatory tone on Iran: Richard L. Armitage, *U.S. Policy and Iran. Testimony before the Senate Foreign Relations Committee* 28 October 2003 [4 April 2005]; available from http://www.state.gov/s/d/former/armitage/remarks/25682.htm.

166   In a testimony before the Senate International Relations Committee in 2003 Armitage struck a demonstratively conciliatory tone on Iran: Ibid.

167   Steven R. Weisman, "Bush Aides Divided on Confronting Iran Over A-Bomb," *New York Times*, 21 September 2004, A3. Bolton took a similar position in the administration's internal deliberations about how to approach the nuclear threat from North Korea: Glenn Kessler, "U.S. Has Shifting Script on N. Korea; Administration Split as New Talks Near," *Washington Post*, 7 December 2003, A25.

168   Weisman, "Bush Aides Divided on Confronting Iran Over A-Bomb." Bolton took a similar position in the administration's internal deliberations about how to approach the nuclear threat from North Korea: Kessler, "U.S. Has Shifting Script on N. Korea; Administration Split as New Talks Near."

169   Elise Labott, *Armitage, Bolton often clashed, aide says. Says U.N. nominee a source of tension at State Department* CNN.com, 10 May 2005 [7 May 2006]; available from http://www.cnn.com/2005/POLITICS/05/10/bolton.armitage/index.html.

170   Cf. Sonni Efron, "U.S. Options Few in Feud With Iran; Alarmed at Tehran's nuclear ambitions, Washington for now can only watch and wait," *Los Angeles Times*, 13 December 2004, A1.

171   Kessler and Slevin, "Rice Fails to Repair Rifts.", Rothkopf, *Running the World* 393.

172   Guy Dinmore, "Hawks and pragmatists to mix on Rice's team," *Financial Times (London)*, 17 January 2005, 8, Meghan L. O'Sullivan, "The Politics of Dismantling Containment," *Washington Quarterly* 24, no. 1 (2001) 67-76.

looking into more confrontational policy options. [173] During the first term of the Bush administration, Rice focused her role on advising the President and less on using the NSC staff to shape foreign policy.[174]

The following preliminary picture emerges with regard to the bureaucratic process of formulating U.S. Iran policy during the first Bush administration: As a direct result of opposing policy preferences within President Bush's international security team in combination with the President's reluctance to tip the balance in favor of either side, the administration found it difficult to agree on a definitive approach towards Iran. The primary battle over Iran policy was fought between *Chiefs* in the Pentagon and the Department of State. In this dispute, the Vice President's office and the National Security Advisor played the roles of swing voters.

2.2.   Analysis of U.S. Iran Policy (2003-2004)

With the policy preferences and roles of the most influential personalities and organizational stumbling blocks of the first Bush administration in mind, let us now trace how U.S. Iran policy developed in 2003 and 2004 from the Liberalism I point of view. The revelations about Iran's clandestine nuclear activities, confirmed by U.S. authorities in December 2002, increased suspicions about the country's pursuit of nuclear weapons across the entire administration.[175] But a coherent policy had yet to emerge. Prior to the publication of the new intelligence, Deputy National Security Adviser Stephen Hadley was tasked by the President to oversee the preparation of a National Security Presidential Directive (NSPD) which would lay down the principles of U.S. Iran policy.[176] The interagency process of formulating NSPDs on critical national security issues is an essential ingredient to making and implementing U.S. foreign policy. As Jeffrey Richelson argued, NSPDs have three key merits:

> "Putting down on paper presidential decisions in the national security area has several virtues. First, it forces a single statement of policy in a particular area. Second, it provides a means to communicate that decision to agencies which will be responsible for implementing it. Third, in the case of disputes as to what the policy is the directives can be used as a point of reference."[177]

---

[173]   Steven R. Weisman, "Bush Confronts New Challenge On Issue of Iran," *New York Times*, 19 November 2004, A1.
[174]   Kessler and Slevin, "Rice Fails to Repair Rifts."
[175]   Dana Priest, "Iran's Emerging Nuclear Plant Poses Test for U.S.," *Washington Post*, 29 July 2002, A01.
[176]   Gellman and Linzer, "Unprecedented Peril Forces Tough Calls."
[177]   Jeffrey Richelson, *Presidential Directives on National Security from Truman to George W. Bush* (Volume II) Digital National Security Archive, [12 June 2006]; available from http://nsarchive.chadwyck.com/pdessayx.htm.

The opposing views of the Pentagon and the State Department on Iran, however, essentially blocked the conclusion of a definitive approach and its codification in a presidential directive.[178] In the struggle over coherent policy, Condoleezza Rice was supportive of the State Department in thwarting efforts from the Secretary of Defense and others in the Pentagon's leadership to make measures supporting "regime change" in Iran official policy.[179] As the New York Times reported in May 2003, the Pentagon favored approaches which included "the possibility of a military strike against the Natanz facility and more active support of Iranian opposition groups."[180] On the other hand, leading State Department officials were in favor of trying to engage Iran and to propose incentives (such as U.S. agreement to Iran's entry into the World Trade Organization) in order to test whether Tehran would be willing to give up the pursuit of nuclear weapons.[181]

While the State Department did not succeed in making an American version of "engagement" official policy, it had managed to enter into a secret dialogue with Iran earlier. In the aftermath of the terrorist attacks of 9/11, a form of "limited engagement" between State Department officials and Iranian officials evolved.[182] The officials were meeting regularly to discuss issues of common concern on neutral territory in Geneva. Judging from the Liberalism I perspective, we can assume that the Pentagon and the State Department held different preferences regarding the future of these talks. Probably in an attempt to seek broader support for its contacts with Iran, the State Department officially confirmed the existence of the so-called Geneva contact group in May 2003.[183] The dialogue had evolved beyond the initial issues of Afghanistan to include the situation in Iraq, Middle East peace efforts, and even Tehran's involvement in terrorism.[184] But despite Washington's increased suspicions about Iran's nuclear program, negotiators were instructed not to discuss the nuclear issue with their Iranian counterparts.[185] The Pentagon appeared eager to restrict further engagement with Iran. In April 2003, Donald Rumsfeld accused Iran of hostile acts against U.S. troops in Iraq and threatened retaliation against the regime.[186] This confrontational statement, which the neorealist perspective attributed to an American position of strength after the relatively

---

[178] Gellman and Linzer, "Unprecedented Peril Forces Tough Calls."
[179] Steven R. Weisman, "As Iraq was escalates, so does anxiety over Iran," *International Herald Tribune*, 21 September 2004, 1.
[180] Steven R. Weisman, "Threats and Responses: Washington; U.S. Demands that Iran Turn Over Qaeda Agents and Join Saudi Inquiry," *New York Times*, 25 May 2003, A9.
[181] Gellman and Linzer, "Unprecedented Peril Forces Tough Calls."
[182] For background information on secret U.S.-Iranian cooperation through the so-called "Geneva Group" see: Pollack, *The Persian Puzzle* 346-374.
[183] Robin Wright, "U.S. In 'Useful' Talks with Iran. The meetings have focused recently on Iraq, Middle East peace efforts and terrorism," *Los Angeles Times*, 13 May 2003, 4. The talks were the first publicly acknowledged links between the U.S. and Iran since the break-off of diplomatic relations in 1979. Ibid.
[184] Ibid.
[185] Gellman and Linzer, "Unprecedented Peril Forces Tough Calls."
[186] Harnden, "US accuses Syria and Iran of 'hostile acts'."

easy military victory in Iraq, now emerges as the view of one of the Bush administration's most influential *Chiefs*. From the Pentagon's point of view, Iran appeared as an "enemy" within the context of the Iraq War.

At the time of Rumsfeld's accusations, Tehran sent a proposal to Washington suggesting comprehensive talks between the two countries about all outstanding issues of concern—including the nuclear program.[187] In the absence of diplomatic relations between the United States and Iran, the Iranians asked the Swiss ambassador to forward the proposal to Washington.[188] According to former Bush administration officials, the agenda explicitly acknowledged that Iran would have to address its support for terrorism and calm international concerns about its nuclear program.[189] As we would expect from the Liberalism I perspective, Colin Powell and Richard Armitage were inclined to explore the Iranian offer and test the sincerity of the Iranian regime. [190] But administration hardliners remained deeply averse to deal with Tehran in a way that would legitimize the regime. [191] After internal deliberations, the Bush administration declined the offer and complained to the Swiss ambassador that he had overstepped his mandate.[192]

The reporting of several daily newspapers provides ample evidence of how the bureaucratic turf war between the Pentagon, the Vice President's office and the State Department continued to play out during the first Bush administration. The all-pervasive clash among key players in the cabinet largely forced the United States government to determine Iran policy in an *ad hoc* fashion. [193] A critical contentious issue centered around the Mujahedeen-e-Khalq (MEK), the militant Iranian dissident organization listed as a terrorist organization by the State Department. The organization's explicitly stated goal was the overthrow of the Iranian regime—which made it a potential ally for those in the Bush cabinet seeking regime change. Since the MEK was based in Iraq and its members had come under U.S. control following the invasion of the country, its future role and purpose had to be agreed upon inside the Bush administration. While officials in the Pentagon and the Vice President's office contemplated to use the MEK in some form against the Iranian regime in the future, Condoleezza Rice and Colin Powell succeeded in ordering that no political contacts be

---

[187]   Gellman and Linzer, "Unprecedented Peril Forces Tough Calls."

[188]   The Swiss were—and still are—the "protecting power" of Washington's interests in Iran.

[189]   Council on Foreign Relations, *Interview with Flynt Leverett: Bush Administration 'Not Serious' About Dealing With Iran* 31 March 2006 [13 June 2006]; available from http://www.cfr.org/publication/10326/.

[190]   Flynt L. Leverett, "Iran: The Gulf Between Us," *New York Times*, 24 January 2006, A21, Lawrence B. Wilkerson, *The White House Cabal* 25 October 2005 [12 June 2006]; available from http://www.latimes.com/news/opinion/commentary/la-oe-wilkerson25oct25,0,7455395.story?coll=la-news-comment-opinions.

[191]   Leverett, "Iran: The Gulf Between Us.", Wilkerson, *The White House Cabal*.

[192]   Leverett, "Iran: The Gulf Between Us."

[193]   Weisman, "As Iraq was escalates, so does anxiety over Iran."

established with the organization shortly after the invasion of Iraq.[194] When a terrorist attack in the Saudi capital Riyadh killed 34 people, including nine Americans, in May 2003, the MEK controversy within the Bush administration resurfaced. [195] Washington received intelligence about the involvement of al-Qaeda members in the attack that were based on Iranian territory and sent a message to Iran demanding their turnover.[196] Iran reportedly offered to strike a deal. In exchange for handing over the al-Qaeda personnel Washington would have to expel the MEK that was still stationed in Iraq and remained under U.S. control.[197] But Bush administration hardliners succeeded in preventing the deal and forced the State Department to suspend its informal contacts with Iranian officials in Geneva.[198] Instead of setting the stage for a greater role of secret diplomacy, the Bush administration seemed to embark on a more confrontational path.

During the summer of 2003, when the E3 started to negotiate the 'Tehran Declaration' with Iran, diplomacy at the IAEA received greater attention from the Bush administration. Promoting U.S. national interests in Vienna was a key responsibility of Undersecretary of State for Arms Control John Bolton. The E3's conditional engagement approach was directly antithetical to Bolton's policy preferences.[199] Instead of negotiations with Iran, Bolton promoted the country's referral to the UN Security Council to set the stage for punitive measures against the country. In order to have a freer hand in pressuring IAEA board members to support his aggressive stance, he even kept information away from Colin Powell and Condoleezza Rice.[200]

But the E3 engagement effort was also met with skepticism from Bolton's superiors at the State Department. Colin Powell stated that while the U.S. was not looking for a confrontation with Tehran, the signing of the NPT's additional protocol was not enough to assure Iranian compliance with its obligations and Deputy Secretary of State Richard Armitage conditioned the improvement of U.S.-Iranian relations on Tehran's cooperation with the IAEA and an end to its support for

---

194   Glenn Kessler, "U.S. Eyes Pressing Uprising In Iran; Officials Cite Al Qaeda Links, Nuclear Program," *Washington Post*, 25 May 2003, A01, Pollack, *The Persian Puzzle* 360.

195   Flynt Leverett in: PBS News Hour, *Threat From Tehran?* See also: Pollack, *The Persian Puzzle* 345-351.

196   Weisman, "Threats and Responses: Washington; U.S. Demands that Iran Turn Over Qaeda Agents and Join Saudi Inquiry."

197   Pollack, *The Persian Puzzle* 360. Washington signed a ceasefire agreement with the MEK after disarming it following the invasion of Iraq in 2003.

198   Kessler, "U.S. Eyes Pressing Uprising In Iran." See also: Weisman, "Threats and Responses: Washington; U.S. Demands that Iran Turn Over Qaeda Agents and Join Saudi Inquiry."

199   Dafna Linzer, "Bolton Often Blocked Information, Officials Say. Iran, IAEA Matters Were Allegedly Kept From Rice, Powell," *Washington Post*, 18 April 2005, A04. Bolton also chiefly promoted Mohamed ElBaradei's replacement and clashed about ways to further this goal with Colin Powell. Cf. Dafna Linzer, "IAEA Leader's Phone Tapped. U.S. Pores Over Transcripts to Try to Oust Nuclear Chief," *Washington Post*, 12 December 2004, A01.

200   Linzer, "Bolton Often Blocked Information, Officials Say. Iran, IAEA Matters Were Allegedly Kept From Rice, Powell." Bolton also chiefly promoted Mohamed ElBaradei's replacement and clashed about ways to further this goal with Colin Powell. Cf. Linzer, "IAEA Leader's Phone Tapped. U.S. Pores Over Transcripts to Try to Oust Nuclear Chief."

terrorism.[201] Similarly, President Bush cautioned that the turnover of al-Qaeda personnel to the U.S. would remain a crucial precondition for any rapprochement.[202]

In late December 2003, a devastating earthquake around the ancient Iranian city of Bam allowed the Bush administration to reach out to the Iranian people in a non-committal way. The White House and the State Department announced steps to ease the transfer of money and materiel for humanitarian relief efforts in Iran, otherwise banned by U.S. sanctions.[203] Colin Powell signaled that Washington discussed the possibility of resuming behind-the-scenes talks with Tehran that had been suspended in May 2003.[204] But as the Liberalism I perspective helps to highlight, the signs of a renewed internal debate had little room to evolve into a new approach. While the State Department continued to work towards facilitating dialogue between Iran and the U.S.—in late January 2004, it granted a request by the Iranian UN ambassador Javad Zarif to travel to Washington, D.C. to meet with a bipartisan congressional group—administration hardliners continued to block policies going into the direction of engagement.[205]

In the year of the presidential elections, instead of urging a new and coherent approach, President Bush repeated the mantra of U.S. demands vis-à-vis Tehran. In his State of the Union Address 2004 Bush reiterated that before Washington would show any diplomatic flexibility, the Iranian regime would have to: "listen to the voices of those who long for freedom, […] turn over al-Qaida that are in their custody, and […] abandon their nuclear weapons program."[206] The presidential election campaign also accentuated foreign policy differences between Republicans and Democrats. In a speech at the Air Force Academy graduation in June the President refuted the mounting criticism of the Iraq War and defended the core of his foreign policy.

> "Some who call themselves realists question whether the spread of democracy in the Middle East should be any concern of ours. But the realists, in this case, have lost contact with a fundamental reality. […] America is always more secured, when freedom is on the march."[207]

Meanwhile, Senator John Kerry, the Democratic presidential candidate, and his running mate John Edwards, announced that, if elected, they would take a more active role in either joining European

---

[201] U.S. Department of State, *Interview by The Washington Post*. And: Armitage, *U.S. Policy and Iran. Testimony before the Senate Foreign Relations Committee*.

[202] The White House, *Roundtable Interview of the President by the Press Pool, Aboard Air Force One, En Route Canberra, Australia*.

[203] Robin Wright, "U.S. Makes Overture To Iran. Sen. Dole Could Head Aid Mission," *Washington Post*, 2 January 2004, A01.

[204] Robin Wright, "U.S. Warms to Prospect of New Talks with Iran," *Washington Post*, 30 December 2003, A01.

[205] In November 2002 the same initiative by the State Department had been blocked by administration "hardliners." Robin Wright, "Iranian Envoy a Guest of Congress; Similar Visit was Blocked in 2002," *Washington Post*, 29 January 2004, A17.

[206] The White House, *President's Remarks to the Press Pool, Brooks County Airport, Falfurrias, Texas* 1 January 2004 [7 April 2006]; available from http://www.whitehouse.gov/news/releases/2004/01/20040101.html.

[207] The White House, *Remarks by the President at the United States Air Force Academy Graduation Ceremony* 22 June 2004 [5 May 2005]; available from http://www.whitehouse.gov/news/releases/2004/06/20040602.html.

negotiating efforts or talking to the Iranians directly.[208]

The NSPD, which was intended to provide the administration with a unified approach, remained unfinished and unsigned by the President.[209] Because many of the policy questions continued to be contested internally, the Bush administration continued to formulate its approach towards Iran 'on the fly.'[210] In order to develop policy options which could be implemented after the presidential elections, administration hawks increasingly discussed military measures to topple the Iranian regime.[211] In June 2004, a senior Bush administration official from the camp of administration hardliners asserted that the U.S. would "mount a concerted attempt to overturn the regime in Iran if President Bush is elected for a second term," expressing the hope that this intervention "would foment a revolt against the ruling theocracy by Iran's hugely dissatisfied population."[212] As a liberal foreign policy theory I perspective helps to clarify, these calls showed a growing impatience in hawkish circles in the administration with the European negotiating effort, and a desire to finally come up with a distinctly American approach. Some members of the Bush administration began to ridicule Germany, France, and the United Kingdom for being too conciliatory towards the Iranians, calling them "the Tehran three" and naming Jack Straw "Jack of Tehran."[213] If nothing else, this showed that the Bush administration was still split on how to handle Iran and that "the White House [was] pulled in distinctly different directions."[214]

But the internal stalemate on Iran policy continued. The renewed push for "regime change" through covert action remained opposed by Condoleezza Rice and the State Department leaving the administration devoid of a conclusive approach towards Iran.[215]

As the Liberalism I perspective helps to show, a mirror image of these conceptual divisions can be witnessed with regard to the Bush administration's approach to diplomacy at the IAEA. Prior to the September 2004 IAEA meeting in Vienna, Condoleezza Rice tried to bring the irreconcilable camps of "hawks" and "doves" together when she remarked that Iran had to be "isolated in its bad behavior, not quote-unquote, engaged."[216] The statement aimed at steering a middle-course between keeping the diplomatic track open, while conceding to administration hardliners that no rewards

208 Guy Dinmore, "US split over Iranian bid to renew relations," *Financial Times (London)*, 17 March 2004, 1, Glenn Kessler and Robin Wright, "Edwards Says Kerry Plans To Confront Iran On Weapons," *Washington Post*, 30 August 2004, A01.
209 Robin Wright, "U.S. Faces a Crossroads on Iran Policy," *Washington Post*, 19 July 2004, A09.
210 Schmitt, "Pentagon Office in Spying Case Was Focus of Iran Debate."
211 Guy Dinmore, "US debates military strikes on 'nuclear Iran'," *Financial Times (London)*, 16 September 2004, 12.
212 Michael Binyon and Bronwen Maddox, "US sets sights on toppling Iran regime," *The Times of London*, 17 July 2004.
213 Ibid.
214 Wright, "U.S. Faces a Crossroads on Iran Policy."
215 Guy Dinmore, "Presidential rivals take divergent views on Tehran 'atomic threat': Bush is for isolation while Kerry wants to talk," *Financial Times (London)*, 2 September 2004, 7.
216 Dinmore and Smyth, "Support grows for UN showdown with Iran over nuclear programme."

should be offered in advance to any change in Iranian behavior.[217] This somewhat indicisive stance left Washington's efforts to garner support for a U.S.-sponsored resolution that could provide the basis to refer Iran to the UN Security Council, hopelessly unsuccessful and allowed Iran to play a game of "catch-me-if-you-can" with the IAEA and the international community.[218] The resulting absence of constructive American leadership in Vienna also allowed the E3 to conclude their second agreement with Iran on November 14, 2004. The subsequent positive assessment about Tehran's cooperative behavior by the IAEA rendered U.S. diplomatic efforts for immediate UN Security Council involvement fruitless.[219]

2.3.   Main Players in the Second Bush Administration

Let us now take a look at how the make-up of the second Bush administration has affected the policy adjustments vis-à-vis Iran in 2005 and 2006. Seen from a Liberalism I perspective, the cabinet reshuffle following President Bush's re-election on November 2, 2004 inserted a crucial new dynamic into American foreign (and Iran) policy. Initially, Colin Powell's resignation on November 15 seemed to be a drawback for the potential of traditional diplomacy and multilateral coalition-building towards Iran.[220] In his position as Secretary of State, Powell was the leading advocate for (limited) engagement with the country. At the same time, however, he was unable to gain critical influence in shaping policy, mainly due to a lack of support and trust from the President.[221]

National Security Advisor Condoleezza Rice—personally close to and trusted by President Bush—succeeded Powell in the position as chief diplomat. The new Secretary was reportedly "of two minds about the problem [of Iran]."[222] Rice's nomination reflected the President's desire "to take personal control of the government […], especially of departments and agencies that he felt that undermined him in the first four years" and to terminate the permanent fights in his administration on how to approach foreign policy.[223] With Rice's arrival in Foggy Bottom, the State Department was

[217] Ibid.
[218] Linzer, "Iran Negotiates Deal to Curtail Nuclear Work; U.S. Sees Offer as Bid to Stall Sanctions."
[219] Linzer, "U.N. Finds No Nuclear Bomb Program in Iran; Agency Report and Tehran's Deal With Europe Undercut Thougher U.S. Stance."
[220] Allen, "Powell Announced his Resignation; Secretary of State Clashed With Cheney and Rumsfeld; Rice to Succeed Him." See also: John C. Hulsman, "Bush's home run: neocon victory, realist world," *Opendemocracy.com* (23 November 2004).
[221] David E. Sanger and Steven R. Weisman, "Bush seeks to end turf wars on security issues," *International Herald Tribune*, 18 November 2004, 2. See also: David E. Sanger and Steven R. Weisman, "Cabinet Choices Seen as Move For More Harmony and Control," *New York Times*, 16 November 2004, A1.
[222] Weisman, "Bush Confronts New Challenge On Issue of Iran."
[223] Allen, "Powell Announced his Resignation; Secretary of State Clashed With Cheney and Rumsfeld; Rice to Succeed Him." And: Sanger, "Who'd Be In, Who'd Be Out."

enabled to play an increasingly central role in formulating and implementing Iran policy. Remaining personally close to the President, Rice was given greater institutional clout to promote her own views on U.S. foreign policy.

In a broader context, Rice also epitomized a generational change in the Bush administration's foreign policy team that showed a greater confidence in the power of diplomacy.[224] Rice surrounded herself with people who shared the notion that building international coalitions to deal with the Iranian nuclear crisis was a desirable and attainable goal and would further U.S. national interests. The core of the new "inner circle" at the State Department was constituted by Robert Zoellick, who replaced Richard Armitage as Deputy Secretary of State, the former NATO ambassador Nicholas Burns, who became Undersecretary of State for Policy, and Philip Zelikow, a long-time friend of the new Secretary, who came to the department as counselor.[225] Under the new National Security Advisor Stephen Hadley, who had been Rice's deputy before, the NSC continued to matter less on policy issues.[226]

While Condoleezza Rice's promotion as Secretary of State was the most obvious personnel change in Bush's second term cabinet, the removal of influential neoconservatives such as Paul Wolfowitz and Douglas Feith at the Pentagon, as well as of I. Lewis Libby (who had to resign in 2005 amid allegations of leaking confidential information to the media) tilted the administration's foreign policy team in a more pragmatic direction.[227] John Bolton, who had been out of step with the State Department's leadership of Powell and Armitage, was named new U.S. ambassador to the United Nations.[228] It was Condoleezza Rice who took the initiative of sidelining Bolton and removing him from active policy making to carve out more room for diplomacy towards Iran and other national security issues.[229] Despite a relative loss of influence, Dick Cheney and Donald Rumsfeld remained as important and powerful personalities in the background. Especially Cheney had still a say with regard to formulating a policy towards Iran.[230]

Liberalism I highlights another critical change between the first and the second Bush cabinet. The President's growing involvement into formulating foreign policy. After four years of exposure and experience, George Bush became more confident to interject when it came to deciding on issues

[224] James Mann, "The next generation seeks a more diplomatic America," *Financial Times (London)*, 26 April 2005, 19.
[225] Glenn Kessler, "Rice Taps Longtime Colleagues for Inner Circle," *Washington Post*, 7 June 2005, A21.
[226] David J. Rothkopf, "Look Who's Running the World Now," *Washington Post*, 12 March 2006, B01.
[227] Ibid.
[228] Peter Baker and Dafna Linzer, "Policy Shift Felt After Bolton's Departure From State Dept," *Washington Post*, 20 June 2005, A02, Sonni Efron, "Harsh Critic of U.N. Named Ambassador," *Los Angeles Times*, 8 March 2005, A1.
[229] Baker and Linzer, "Policy Shift Felt After Bolton's Departure From State Dept.", Efron, "Harsh Critic of U.N. Named Ambassador." Bolton's replacement, Robert Joseph, was assistant for arms control under Rice and had worked closely with her at the National Security Council during the first term. Dinmore, "Hawks and pragmatists to mix on Rice's team."
[230] Rothkopf, *Running the World* Chapter 12.

relating to Iran policy.[231]

2.4.   Analysis of U.S. Iran Policy (2005-2006)

Against the backdrop of these important changes in the make-up of the second Bush administration, let us now look at their effects on U.S. Iran policy. While President Bush continued and intensified his rhetoric on the necessity of spreading democracy across the Middle East (most notably in his Inaugural and his State of the Union Addresses in early 2005), he also indicated his intentions of reaching out across the Atlantic and working with the European allies to defuse the crisis over Iran.[232] Bush's good working relationship with Condoleezza Rica helped him to draw more extensively on the diplomatic tools, which the State Department provided. It was Rice's mission to look for practical steps that would help restore transatlantic ties which had suffered from the controversial invasion of Iraq. On a mission to Europe in early 2005, Rice refrained from making promises that the U.S. would join E3 negotiations with Iran.[233] As the Liberalism I model helps us understand, President Bush and Rice were looking for diplomatic options on Iran, while the Vice President's Office and the Pentagon still tried to promote more confrontational policies with the ultimate goal of "regime change." Dick Cheney suggested in an interview that Israel might be tempted to use military force against Iran and the Pentagon announced that Washington would sell bunker-busting bombs to Israel.[234] Additionally, civilian planners at Department of Defense were drawing up their own plans to come up with military options on Iran.[235] As Seymour Hersh reported, Donald Rumsfeld ordered to conduct covert military operations inside Iran to accumulate intelligence and targeting information on Iranian nuclear, chemical, and missile sites for potential precision air strikes.[236] Key Pentagon planners remained hopeful that limited air strikes could help bring down the regime by fomenting a new revolution against the ruling elite.[237] Questioned about

---

[231]   Sanger, "Who'd Be In, Who'd Be Out."

[232]   In his Inaugural Address Bush stated: "So it is the policy of the United States to seek and support the growth of democratic movements and institutions in every nation and culture, with the ultimate goal of ending tyranny in our world. This is not primarily the task of arms, though we will defend ourselves and our friends by force of arms when necessary." The White House, *President Sworn-In to Second Term (Inaugural Address 2005)* 20 January 2005 [7 April 2006]; available from http://www.whitehouse.gov/news/releases/2005/01/20050120-1.html. In his State of the Union speech, Bush branded Iran as the "world's primary state sponsor of terror" and directly addressed the Iranian people: "As you stand for your own liberty, America stands with you." The White House, *State of the Union Address by the President.*

[233]   Weisman and Dempsey, "Rice works to bolster ties with Europe.", Wright, "Rice Says U.S. Won't Join Europe in Iran Nuclear Talks."

[234]   Abraham Rabinovich, "Sale of 'bunker busters' seen as a warning to Iran," *Washington Times,* 29 April 2005, A16, David E. Sanger, "Cheney Says Israel Might 'Act First' on Iran," *New York Times,* 21 January 2005, A6.

[235]   Hersh, *Fact: The Coming Wars. What the Pentagon can now do in secret.*

[236]   Ibid.

[237]   Ibid.

these reports, Rumsfeld stated that he had been "amazed at how rapidly the shah fell and the ayatollahs took over"—a statement which clearly suggested that policy related to "regime change" were still under intense debate.[238]

When the President traveled to Europe in February 2005, he announced to consider fully endorsing the E3 diplomatic process and even providing some incentives to Tehran.[239] Liberalism I suggests that the decision to make tactical changes to facilitate a compromise with the Europeans on Iran was made by the President himself. The exact nature and the conditions of U.S. support for the E3, however, were left to the main players in his cabinet to agree upon. As during the first Bush administration there were still two main tribal groupings—the State Department and parts of the National Security Council staff vs. the Pentagon and the Vice President's Office—favoring different approaches. However, the underlying metrics had changed. National Security Advisor Stephen Hadley, Undersecretary of State for Political Affairs Nicholas Burns, members of the Nonproliferation and the Near Eastern bureaus at the State Department, and other NSC staffers emerged as supporters of the European approach of engaging Iran, arguing that with the right mix of incentives, Iran might consent to conclude a long-term agreement with the west.[240] On the other end of the spectrum were the adamant skeptics of engagement. Dick Cheney and Donald Rumsfeld argued that the E3 could not be trusted to support a tougher stance on Iran if negotiations failed.[241] Instead they recommended increased pressure for a UN Security Council referral at the IAEA.[242] A compromise between the two camps was negotiated by Condoleezza Rice and Robert Zoellick who obtained pledges from the E3 to support a UN Security Council referral in the case of a failure of the negotiations.[243] The Bush administration agreed on limited incentives for Iran, which included the dropping of American opposition to Iranian WTO membership and allowing the sale of civilian aircraft parts to the country. The reinvigorated position of the State Department under Rice's and Zoellick's leadership helped to sideline administration's hardliners, who remained unable to force a definitive agreement with regard to a deadline when E3 negotiations with Iran would be declared a failure.[244] Walking a thin line between the two camps, Condoleezza Rice marketed these policy

[238]   Bradley Graham, "U.S. Officials Discout Risk of Iran-Style Rule," *Washington Post*, 7 February 2005, A18.
[239]   Dinmore and Wetzel, "President faces hard sell over Iran policy."
[240]   Lawrence F. Kaplan, "Tehran Twist - Bush's New Iran Policy," *The New Republic*, 28 March 2005.
[241]   Ibid.
[242]   Ibid.
[243]   Robin Wright, "U.S. Wants Guarantees on Iran Effort; Support for U.N. Action Sought if Tehran Does Not Abandon Nuclear Program," *Washington Post*, 4 March 2005, A12, Robin Wright and Peter Baker, "U.S. to Back Europeans on Incentives for Iran; Rice to Announce Shift on Nuclear Issue," *Washington Post*, 11 March 2005, A14.
[244]   While the E3 were arguing in favor of waiting until after the Iranian presidential elections in June, hawks inside the Bush administration were pressing for a quicker decision. Steven R. Weisman, "U.S. chafes at slow pace of nuclear diplomacy," *International Herald Tribune*, 28 March 2005, 1, Robin Wright, "U.S., Allies May Have to Wait Out Iran's Presidential Vote," *Washington Post*, 13 March 2005, A16.

adjustments simply as support for the E3 and avoided talking about the provision of U.S. incentives: "This is not engagement with the Iranians. This is giving to the Europeans more cards to play in their negotiations [...]."[245]

The new approach was supplemented by State Department efforts to implement the President's "freedom agenda" more aggressively.[246] As Liberalism I helps to show, this new mix of pragmatism vis-à-vis the E3 in combination with a new push for promoting democracy around the world flowed from the preferences of President Bush and his good relationship with Condoleezza Rice. Just before the Iranian presidential elections in June 2005, which propelled Mahmoud Ahmadi-Nejad to power, Bush reiterated his support for the Iranian people in their "struggle for freedom" and denounced the regime in Tehran as "men who suppress liberty at home and spread terror across the world."[247] Efforts to support regime opposition inside the country by channeling aid to pro-democracy groups—something which the State Department was traditionally extremely cautious about in order not to anger the Iranian regime—were substantially increased.[248] Despite being conceptually counterproductive, these measures were taken alongside U.S. support for E3 diplomacy.[249] As the Liberalism I perspective highlights, President Bush's decision to coordinate Iran policy more closely with the E3 from February 2005 continued to inform the American position. When Iran rejected the comprehensive European offer that the Bush administration officially supported in August 2005, President Bush kept the door open for further rounds of negotiations.[250] Demonstrating more flexibility herself, Condoleezza Rice even signaled that tactical engagement with Iran on Afghanistan and Iraq could be resumed in the future.[251] In that context, Zalmay Khalilzad, the U.S. ambassador to Iraq, was given the authority to revive the secret talks with the Iranians in Geneva.[252]

The combination of pushing for greater democracy and freedom inside Iran and the pursuit of a diplomatic option to solve the Iranian nuclear crisis became the central theme of the second Bush

---

[245] Efron, "Bush Softens Stance on Iran."

[246] Guy Dinmore, Carola Hoyos, and Gareth Smyth, "US casts doubt on new leader's legitimacy," *Financial Times (London)*, 27 June 2005, 5.

[247] Robin Wright and Michael A. Fletcher, "Bush Denounces Iran's Elections; President Vows to Stand by Citizenry in Struggle for Freedom," *Washington Post*, 1 / June 2005, A18.

[248] Sonni Efron and Mark Mazzetti, "U.S. May Aid Iran Activists," *Los Angeles Times*, 4 March 2004, A1, Steven R. Weisman, "U.S. Expands Aid to Iran's Democracy Advocates Abroad," *New York Times*, 29 May 2005, 8. Other confrontational measures, such as the imposition of economic sanctions, were also considered further. Dafna Linzer, "U.S. Plans New Tool to Halt Spread of Weapons," *Washington Post*, 27 June 2005, A01.

[249] From a Liberalism I perspective we are unable to reach definitive conclusions as to why the conceptual contradiction of support for negotiations with the Iranian regime despite efforts towards a destabilization of that regime occurred.

[250] Linzer, "Bush Cautiously Optimistic as Iran Offers to Negotiate."

[251] James Blitz and Guy Dinmore, "Rice fails to win support for Iran referral to Security Council," *Financial Times (London)*, 17 October 2005, 12.

[252] Ibid.

administration's Iran policy. From the Liberalism I perspective, this elusive policy mix is only explicable if we take into account the different players involved in the game of formulating policy. We can assume that the Vice President's Office (with support from the Pentagon) was eager to see a greater push for democracy in Iran. Simultaneously, President Bush seemed to be convinced to proceed on both tracks, pushing for a democratic Iran and keeping the diplomatic option alive. In his State of the Union Address 2006 he stated:

> "Tonight, let me speak directly to the citizens of Iran: America respects you, and we respect your country. We respect your right to choose your own future and win your own freedom. And our nation hopes one day to be the closest of friends with a free and democratic Iran."[253]

In 2006, the Bush administration increased its efforts to support a 'soft version of regime change.'[254] On February 15, 2006, the State Department requested an additional US$75 million from Congress to advance democracy in Iran by expanding broadcasting, funding nongovernmental organizations (which would channel the money to regime opponents and reformers) and promoting cultural exchanges.[255] Reflecting the President's position, Condoleezza Rice stated that the U.S. had "no problem with the Iranian people" but with the Iranian regime.[256]

At the same time, Washington became more actively engaged in a multilateral effort with the E3, China and Russia.[257] After the referral to the UN Security Council in March 2006, Moscow and Beijing remained opposed to any form of sanctions and Condoleezza Rice concluded that the U.S. had to become more actively engaged in the diplomatic process, before any form of sanctions could be applied with the support of a broad coalition of other countries.[258] While several principals participated in the internal discussions on a new approach towards Iran, the Liberalism I perspective highlights that Rice asserted the State Department's leadership on the issue.[259] It is also

---

[253]   The White House, *State of the Union Address by the President* 31 January 2006 [1 February 2006]; available from http://www.whitehouse.gov/stateoftheunion/2006/index.html.

[254]   Howard LaFranchi, "A bid to foment democracy in Iran," *Christian Science Monitor*, 17 February 2006, 3.

[255]   Glenn Kessler, "Rice Asks for $75 Million to Increase Pressure on Iran," *Washington Post*, 16 February 2006, A01.

[256]   Cit. in: LaFranchi, "A bid to foment democracy in Iran."

[257]   During the time of the deliberations about how to keep the diplomatic track alive the White House chose not to respond to several diplomatic openings from Iran including a letter from the Iranian President Ahmadi-Nejad to President Bush. Guy Dinmore, "Iran ready for high-level talks, US resists," *Financial Times (London)*, 7 April 2006, Hassan Rohani, *Iran's Nuclear Program: The Way Out* Time, 9 May 2006 [6 June 2006]; available from http://www.time.com/time/world/printout/0,8816,1192435,00.html, Karl Vick and Dafna Linzer, "Iran Requests Direct Talks on Nuclear Program," *Washington Post*, 24 May 2006, A01, Karl Vick and Colum Lynch, "No Proposals in Iranian's Letter to Bush, U.S. Says," *Washington Post*, 9 May 2006, A18. Washington also recalled its authorization to Zalmay Khalilzad to engage tactically with the Iranians about the future of Iraq. Julian Borger and Ewen MacAskill, "U-turn by White House as it blocks direct talks with Iran," *The Guardian (London)*, 25 May 2006.

[258]   Washington also worked to press for the application of financial sanctions against Iran outside the UN framework. Dafna Linzer, "U.S. Urges Financial Sanctions on Iran," *Washington Post*, 29 May 2006, A01. Some of these measures showed a first impact in May 2006. Steven R. Weisman, "Pressed By U.S., European Banks Limit Iran Deals," *New York Times*, 22 May 2006, A1.

[259]   Kessler, "Rice Key to Reversal on Iran."

worth noting that the Secretary of Defense—an influential voice on Iran policy during the first term—was not present in the internal debates.[260] At the order of the President, Condoleezza Rice proposed a new policy that included three tracks:

> "The threat of 'coercive measures' through the United Nations; negotiations with Iran that included what Ms. Rice called 'bold' incentives for Iran to give up the production of all nuclear fuel; and a separate set of strategies for American-led economic sanctions against Iran if the Security Council failed to act."[261]

As we can easily discern, Rice's policy proposal aimed at appeasing administration hawks while giving as much support as possible to the multilateral diplomatic approach centering around the E3. After long internal deliberations, Rice was able to announce the administration's readiness to join the E3 in direct negotiations with Iran and offer additional incentives.[262]

While the new policy represented a critical adjustment, the Secretary's actual statement looked more like a compromise following hard bureaucratic battles.[263] The group in favor of multilateral diplomacy and engagement with Tehran apparently gained an important tactical advantage, albeit no outright victory over "regime change" proponents.[264] Rice and the State Department leadership were successful to include 'bold' incentives and the prospect of direct U.S. involvement in multilateral negotiations with Iran, notwithstanding active opposition from the Vice President's office.[265] As Gary Sick noted, this can be seen as "a measurement of how the Cheney forces have been weakened by the unilateralism of Iraq and its aftermath."[266] At the same time, while the offer lacked the aggressive rhetoric of past U.S. statements, it restated Washington's paramount objections to the nature of the Iranian regime. Rice reiterated that a new relationship with Iran "is to be between the peoples of the two countries, not their governments," and dismissed the notion that a "grand bargain" with Iran could be reached.[267]

---

[260] Ibid.

[261] Helene Cooper and David E. Sanger, "A talk at lunch that shifted the stance on Iran," 4 June 2006, A08.

[262] It drew furious criticism from regime change proponents outside the administration. Cf. Frank Gaffney, "Divest Iran," *Washington Times*, 31 May 2006, A16, Michael Ledeen, *Is Bill Clinton Still President?* National Review Online, 7 June 2006 [8 June 2006]; available from http://article.nationalreview.com/?q=ZDg2YzE3ZGQwYWVmYjQ2MDBhZmU0N2NiMzcxYmU2ZGQ=.

[263] As Gary Sick, a former National Security Council staffer on Iran during the Gerald Ford, Jimmy Carter, and Ronald Reagan administrations has stated: "It is important to remember that every word in the statement was weighed and was subject to arguments and objections." Gary Sick, "The US Offer to Iran," *American Iranian Council - AIC Update* 3, no. 45 (June 2006).

[264] Ibid.

[265] Guy Dinmore and Daniel Dombey, *Washington 'hawks' oppose EU3 plan for Iran* Financial Times (London), 23 May 2006 [23 May 2006]; available from http://news.ft.com/cms/s/f5f3b27c-ea7f-11da-9566-0000779e2340.html, David E. Sanger, *For Bush, Talks With Iran Were a Last Resort* New York Times, 1 June 2006 [1 June 2006]; available from http://www.nytimes.com/2006/06/01/world/middleeast/01iran.html?ex=1306814400en=3b41103c1ecf3a8eei=5088partner=rssnytemc=rss&pagewanted=print.

[266] Sick, "The US Offer to Iran."

[267] Rice, *Press Conference on Iran.*

"We believe the Iranian people want a future of freedom and human rights, the right to vote, to run for office, to express their views without fear, and to pursue political causes. We would welcome the progress, prosperity, and freedom of the Iranian people."[268]

From a Liberalism I point of view, this qualification reflects the reluctance and outright opposition by the Vice President's Office and the Pentagon to 'give legitimacy' to the Iranian regime. According to this reading from the Liberalism I perspective, the option of "regime change" remains—although carefully hidden—among Washington's alternative policy preferences. Reports about new U.S. efforts to promote democratic change in Iran support this interpretation.[269] As a former Bush administration official commented, "[d]emocracy promotion is a rubric to get the Europeans behind a more robust policy without calling it regime change."[270] In consequence, a "grand bargain" with the Iranian regime that would aim at resolving all outstanding bilateral issues and involve the prospect of a complete normalization of relations between Washington and Tehran was excluded *ex ante* in Condoleezza Rice's announcement in May 2006.

2.5.   Summary

From the Liberalism I perspective, the Bush administration appeared internally split on Iran. During the time of the first administration, two camps—one favoring diplomacy and engagement, the other favoring confrontation and "regime change"—pulled into different directions regarding the formulation of policy towards the country. A stalemate between the two factions prevented the emergence of a coherent approach. As the President remained indecisive on Iran during his first term, policy on the issue was determined in an *ad hoc* fashion. Bush became more actively involved, however, after his re-election in November 2004. The President's personnel decisions for his second-term cabinet reflected his desire to encourage more coherence of U.S. foreign policy. Bush chose to promote his trusted National Security Advisor as Secretary of State, thereby enabling the State Department to become more dominant in shaping U.S. foreign policy. Colin Powell and Richard Armitage, although willing to look into options for engaging Iran, lacked the President's support during the first term. Additionally, John Bolton had internally worked against his superiors as Undersecretary of State for Arms Control. Rather than showing loyalty to the traditionally realist

---

[268] Ibid.

[269] Laura Rozen, "U.S. Moves to Weaken Iran," *Los Angeles Times*, 19 May 2006, A6.

[270] The quote can be found in: Guy Dinmore and Gareth Smyth, "US and UK develop democracy strategy for Iran," *Financial Times (London)*, 22 April 2006, 9.

leadership of the Department of State, he espoused neoconservative views on Iran, allying himself with the hawkish camp of the administration of Cheney and Rumsfeld.

As the Liberalism I perspective highlights, Condoleezza Rice's promotion can be primarily seen as an assertion of presidential power.[271] Rice's sway on policy resulted from her loyal relationship with the President and she was promoted to overcome the "fractious, even dysfunctional" national security team of the first term.[272] Rice still had to deal with internal opposition to the idea of engaging Iran and tried to bridge the divide between engagement and regime change proponents by carving out a middle course.[273] As National Security Advisor during the first term, Rice was too weak to mediate between the realist and pragmatic camp at the State Department and hawkish circles in the Pentagon and the Vice President's office.

As John Hulsman has stated, "if the first term can be summed up as dominated by the neo-conservatives, the second is much more of a balance of power."[274] From this perspective, the diplomatic offer to Iran from May 2006, although a significant adjustment in comparison to the policy of the first Bush administration, is 'neither fish nor fowl.' Its inherently contradictory messages are reflective of the difficulties of Bush's second national security cabinet to carve out a coherent strategy towards Iran.

---

[271] Sanger and Weisman, "Cabinet Choices Seen as Move For More Harmony and Control."

[272] FT, "Dangerous liaisons in US foreign policy: President Bush's second-term cabinet marches in lockstep," *Financial Times (London)*, 20 November 2004, 12.

[273] Peter Baker, "The Security Adviser Who Wants the Role, Not the Stage," 29 January 2006, A04.

[274] John C. Hulsman, *Beyond the neocons: ethical realism and America's future* Opendemocracy.com, 21 September 2006 [23 September 2006]; available from http://www.opendemocracy.net/democracy-americanpower/neocons_3925.jsp.

3.   Liberalism II: The Influence of Germany

The Liberalism I model opened up the black box of the Bush administration's decision-making process on Iran. The liberal perspective enabled us to see that a stalemate between powerful *Chiefs* in the Bush cabinet blocked the conclusion of a coherent approach during the first term, while personnel changes in the second term and greater personal involvement of the President increased the odds for transatlantic policy coordination and multilateral diplomacy on Iran.

Building on these findings, Liberalism II has two additional goals. First, we can validate the analysis made on the basis of Liberalism I if we are able to prove that Germany's influence on Iran policy during the first Bush administration remained insignificant. Consequently, if we are able to document attempts from Berlin to influence U.S. Iran policy between 2003 and 2004, we should also be able to demonstrate that these attempts were futile due to the dysfunctional make-up of the first Bush administration's national security team. Additionally, Liberalism II seeks to prove that German attempts to influence U.S. Iran policy during the second Bush administration, may have had greater success primarily due to a reinvigorated role of the State Department and greater personal involvement of President Bush.

3.1.   Introduction to German Iran Policy

Before we analyze U.S. Iran policy from the Liberalism II perspective, let us take a closer look at the rationale behind German Iran policy and the motives to seek influence on the Bush administration's approach towards the country.

During the aftermath of the Iraq War in the the summer of 2003, Germany became actively involved in forging a new European approach towards Iran. While Berlin agreed with the assessment of its European allies and the U.S. that Tehran was determined to acquire the capabiltiy to build nuclear weapons, it insisted—unlike Washington at the time—on Iran's right to manage civilian nuclear technology.[275] In order to persuade the country to "clarify" the suspicions of the international community, Berlin proposed a strategy of combining diplomatic pressure with

---

[275] FAS, "Auswärtiges Amt: Teheran will sich Atomwaffen beschaffen," *Frankfurter Allgemeine Sonntagszeitung*, 22 June 2003, 2. See also: FR, "Zum Umsturz mag Berlin die Iraner nicht aufrufen. Bundesregierung hofft auf Einlenken Teherans beim Atomprogramm, Zweifel am Einfluss Khatamis wachsen," *Frankfurter Rundschau*, 20 June 2003, 6.

economic incentives.[276] Since Germany was uncertain about Washington's intentions towards Iran, this strategy had to be implemented mainly with the help of its European allies.[277] In Berlin's view, the American doctrine of preventive warfare (misleadingly called "preemptive warfare" by the Bush administration)[278] had to be countered by alternative European concepts.[279] Berlin was eager to increase the EU's profile in security affairs and to demonstrate the viability of the new (albeit amorphous) concept of "effective multilateralism."[280] The *ad hoc* character of the E3 approach of conditional engagement with Iran—which developed during the summer of 2003—reflected Foreign Minister Joschka Fischer's conviction that "in case of need a group of countries has to advance outside the framework of the treaties"[281] and that "the big three have to be united if the EU wants to be successful."[282] The October 21, 2003 'Tehran Declaration' took into account Germany's demand that Iran should be allowed access to civilian nuclear technology after verifiably foregoing possible military uses.[283] The negotiations with Iran also echoed Berlin's desire to embed the question of Iran's nuclear program into the larger context of promoting regional cooperative security arrangements in the Middle East.[284]

3.2.   The First Bush Administration (2003-2004)

In light of these observations it comes as no surprise that policy coordination between Germany and the United States on Iran and German influence on the Bush administration's Iran policy remained very limited in 2003. Principally, Berlin perceived Iran as an issue that had to be dealt with

---

[276]   FAS, "Auswärtiges Amt: Teheran will sich Atomwaffen beschaffen."

[277]   FR, "Zum Umsturz mag Berlin die Iraner nicht aufrufen."

[278]   For further information of the meaning of preemption vs. prevention see footnore: 17.

[279]   Clemens Verenkotte, *Das Ende der friedlichen Gesellschaft. Deutschlands Illusionen im globalen Krieg* (München: Droemer/Knaur, 2005) 57.

[280]   Joschka Fischer, "Die Rekonstruktion des Westens. Außenminister Fischer über Europa, Amerika und die gemeinsamen strategischen Aufgaben," *Frankfurter Allgemeine Zeitung*, 6 March 2004, 9. See also: Auswärtiges Amt, *"Der Nahe und Mittlere Osten - Überlegungen aus europäischer Sicht" - Rede von Bundesaußenminister Fischer auf der Herzliya Konferenz* 12 December 2003 [5 May 2006]; available from http://www.auswaertiges-amt.de/diplo/de/Infoservice/Presse/Reden/2003/031217-FischerNaherMittlererOsten.html.

[281]   Auswärtiges Amt, *"Notfalls muss in der EU eine Gruppe vorangehen" - Interview von Bundesaußenminister Fischer zur gemeinsamen europäischen Außen- und Sicherheitspolitik im Handelsblatt* 3 April 2003 [7 May 2006]; available from http://www.auswaertiges-amt.de/diplo/de/Infoservice/Presse/Interviews/2003/030403-Handelsblatt,templateId=html.html. [Translated from German.]

[282]   Auswärtiges Amt, *Interview mit Bundesaußenminister Fischer zu verschiedenen außenpolitischen Themen in der "Stuttgarter Zeitung"(Auszug)* 27 October 2003 [7 May 2006]; available from http://www.auswaertiges-amt.de/diplo/de/Infoservice/Presse/Interviews/2003/031027-StuttgarterZeitung,templateId=html.html. [Translated from German.]

[283]   Press Release Germany Info, *Agreed Statement at the End of a Visit to the Islamic Republic of Iran by the Foreign Ministers of Britain, France And Germany* 21 October 2003 [16 April 2006]; available from http://www.germany.info/relaunch/info/press/releases/pr_10_21_03.htm.

[284]   Ibid.

in close coordination with the Americans.[285] But the main transatlantic link on the issue, Joschka Fischer's working relationship with his U.S. counterpart Colin Powell, remained ineffective. Powell's political influence in Washington was undermined not only by Dick Cheney and Donald Rumsfeld, but also by his Under Secretary of State for Arms Control, who tried to bully Germany and other European countries to support Iran's referral to the UN Security Council.[286] John Bolton was avowedly opposed to any form of engagement and dedicated to thwarting U.S. moves in support of the negotiation process which Germany initiated in conjunction with France and the UK.[287] Simultaneously, Gerhard Schröder's strained personal relationship with President Bush prevented any meaningful impact on the issue.[288] However, even given better "chemistry" between the two leaders, it seemed unlikely that President Bush, who remained in the background on foreign policy issues during his first term, would have allowed for greater coordination.

There is another reason why greater European influence on U.S. Iran policy did not materialize during the early stages of E3-Iranian negotiations. It was Colin Powell, after all, who criticized the E3 for being too soft on Iran in the fall of 2003. Iran was able to keep the E3 from reaching a common approach with the U.S. by attaining assurances that Germany, France and the UK would oppose pressure from other countries (especially the United States) to refer the issue to the UN Security Council.[289]

In 2004, Iranian non-compliance with the provisions of the 'Tehran Declaration' slightly facilitated transatlantic coordination. While senior officials from Germany, France, and the UK tried to avoid a failure of the agreement by holding emergency talks with the Iranian side in Vienna, they simultaneously joined Canada, Australia, and the U.S. in backing an IAEA resolution censuring Iran for its hesitant cooperation.[290] In late March, the German, French, and British governments issued parallel statements saying that Iranian intentions to restart the uranium conversion facility in Isfahan would send "the wrong signal about Iranian willingness to implement a suspension of nuclear-enrichment related activities."[291] In a demonstration of unity, the European Union officially started to support E3 negotiations and conditioned the conclusion of the European-Iranian Trade and

---

[285] Joschka Fischer, *Europe and the Future of the Transatlantic Relations, Speech at Princeton University* Germany.info, 20 November 2003 [13 May 2005]; available from http://germany.info/relaunch/politics/speeches/112003.html.

[286] Baker and Linzer, "Policy Shift Felt After Bolton's Departure From State Dept."

[287] Ibid.

[288] For an excellent overview of the strained personal relationship between Schröder and Bush see: Szabo, *Parting Ways*.

[289] Mark Landler, "U.N. Atom Agency Gives Iran Both a Slap and a Pass," *New York Times*, 27 November 2003, A22. Hence, the E3 opposed the U.S. push for UN action at the board of governors meeting in November 2003. Weisman, "U.S. acquiesces to allies on new Iran resolution; Nuclear issue will not be referred to UN."

[290] Traynor, "Europe's nuclear deal with Iran faces collapse." And: Busse, "Beratungen über Iran-Resolution; Widerstand gegen europäisch-amerikanischen Entwurf.", The Economist, *Iran, Libya and nukes* 13 March 2004 [12 May 2006]; available from http://www.economist.com/world/africa/displaystory.cfm?story_id=E1_NVDPDGN.

[291] Ewen MacAskill, "Iran's nuclear facility erodes diplomatic victory," *The Guardian (London)*, 1 April 2004, 12.

Cooperation Agreement (TCA) on progress in the fields of human rights, political reform, and the support of terrorism.[292]

Iran's continuing lack of cooperation with the IAEA in June 2004 facilitated transatlantic cooperation in Vienna. German, French, and British officials at the IAEA drafted a strong worded resolution with support from the U.S., which stopped short of declaring Iran in breach with its obligations under the NPT.[293] As the Liberalism II perspective helps to show, however, this coordination effort was short-lived. In July, Germany, France, and British officials met with their Iranian counterparts on the level of political directors in Paris to discuss measures on how to salvage the 'Tehran Declaration.' Germany effectively tried to mediate between the American pressure for a tougher approach and Iranian reluctance to full and transparent cooperation.[294] During a new round of negotiations in Paris the E3 sought to establish "objective guarantees" with regard to the peaceful nature of Iran's nuclear program.[295] The most critical question that emerged was whether Iran should be allowed to have control over the full nuclear fuel cycle. The E3 proposed that western powers and Russia would guarantee a supply of nuclear fuel in return of Iran renouncing its control of the full fuel cycle.[296] When Iran announced its intention to terminate its commitment to the 'Tehran Declaration' on August 1, 2004 Berlin concluded that would abrogate the agreement for domestic political reasons.[297] Additionally, Germany assumed that, after the threat of a UN Security Council referral had been stopped and the U.S. was seemingly bogged down in Iraq, the Iranian regime had gotten bolder and now desired the second part of the deal, the transfer of technology from Europe, to be realized earlier.[298] As the Liberalism II model helps to show, Germany was caught in the midst between maintaining the diplomatic track with Iran and securing greater support from Washington. Consequently, when Iranian diplomats presented a "wish list" for nuclear dual use technology during an E3-Iranian meeting in late July, Germany warned Iran not

---

[292] Judy Dempsey, "Brussel urges Iran to reform or face bar on trade talks revival," *Financial Times (London)*, 4 May 2004, 9. Later that year, the EU's High Representative for Foreign and Security Policy, Javier Solana, became involved in the negotiation process.

[293] Dafna Linzer and Peter Slevin, "U.N Agency Rebukes Iran on Nuclear Activity; Broken Promises on Disclosure Cited," *Washington Post*, 19 June 2004, A01.

[294] Rudolph Chimelli, "Neue Gespräche über Irans Atomprogramm," *Süddeutsche Zeitung*, 29. July 2004, 8.

[295] Jo Johnson and Gareth Smyth, "Europe trio seeks guarantee on Iran nuclear policy," *Financial Times (London)*, 30 July 2004, 11.

[296] Ibid. After President Bush's reelection, this idea found support in the White House and the State Department. Weisman, "U.S. Reviewing European Proposal for Iran."

[297] dpa/Reuters, "Iran kündigt Atomabkommen mit Europäern," *Süddeutsche Zeitung*, 2 August 2004, 6. Nikolas Busse, "Berlin abwartend im Atomstreit mit Iran," *Frankfurter Allgemeine Zeitung*, 3 August 2004, 4.

[298] Busse, "Berlin abwartend im Atomstreit mit Iran.", Wolfgang Proissl, "Unwiderstehliches Angebot; Nur wenn Deutschland, Frankreich und Großbritannien mit Russland und den USA kooperieren, können sie Irans Atomprogramm ohne Krieg stoppen," *Financial Times Deutschland*, 16 September 2004, 35.

to "miscalculate."[299] After Tehran continued to overplay its cards in 2004, however, Germany sought to involve the U.S. more openly and pressure Iran to cooperate with the IAEA. In September 2004, the E3 agreed to threaten Iran's referral to the UN Security Council.[300] Berlin increased the pressure on Iran by stating that its nuclear activities were "extremely alarming" and that a nuclear arms race in the Middle East would be a "nightmare scenario."[301] As the Liberalism II perspective shows, Berlin's primary goal was to get Iran to return to the negotiating table. Germany tried to avoid 'too much pressure' from the U.S. to prevent a blowback that would make Tehran even less willing to cooperate.[302]

As the Liberalism II model highlights, Germany had little room for influencing U.S. Iran policy. It remained too concerned with the negative effects of U.S. policies and remained itself too inflexible to serve as a transatlantic bridge. At the end of 2004, the context for transatlantic policy coordination started to change. The U.S. presidential elections brought a new dynamic into Iran diplomacy and opened up new channels to influence American foreign policy. As the Liberalism II perspective helps to show, Germany perceived the prospects of new leadership in Washington as an opportunity to forge a comon approach towards Iran according to its preference of combining "carrots" and "sticks." Since the outcome of the elections was too close to call, Germany reached out to the U.S. by holding high-level meetings on Iran with the White House as well as with representatives from democratic presidential challenger John Kerry's camp. [303] During these discussions, German diplomats brought up the idea of a coordinated transatlantic approach.[304] Since the E3 were convinced that incentives such diplomatic recognition from the U.S. and talks about regional security issues had to be part of a new offer to Iran in order to succeed, Washington had to be brought on board.[305] In October 2004, Germany tried to win U.S. support for a "last-ditch approach, not more pressure, but a mix with a package and incentives." [306] The offer which Germany put forward for discussion intended to supply Iran with nuclear fuel for its civilian reactors in exchange for Tehran's agreement to give up its pursuit of a full nuclear fuel cycle.[307] Yet

---

[299] Associated Press, "Iran fordert Zugang zu waffenfähiger Atomtechnologie - "Wunschliste" an EU-Staaten," *AP Worldstream - German*, 9 August 2004.

[300] Ewen MacAskill, Kasra Naji, and Chris McGreal, "UK sets Iran deadline to end nuclear bomb work," *The Guardian (London)*, 9 September 2004, 2.

[301] Horst Bacia, "Außenminister uneinig über Vorgehen gegen Iran; Fischer: Kann Fall für den Sicherheitsrat werden," *Frankfurter Allgemeine Zeitung*, 6 September 2004, 8, MacAskill, Naji, and McGreal, "UK sets Iran deadline to end nuclear bomb work."

[302] Linzer, "No Progress in Nuclear Talks with Iran; U.N. Discussions Likely After European Effort, Powell Says.", Weisman, "Allies Resist U.S. Efforts to Pressure Iran on Arms."

[303] Guy Dinmore, "Europeans urge Bush to adopt Kerry's line on Iran," *Financial Times (London)*, 2 October 2004, 6.

[304] Ibid. These discussions probably occurred for the first time at such high levels.

[305] Weisman, "Bush Confronts New Challenge On Issue of Iran."

[306] Dinmore, "Europeans urge Bush to adopt Kerry's line on Iran."

[307] Ibid.

these discussions remained fruitless. Liberalism II helps to validate the analysis from Liberalism I. The hawkish circles of the Bush administration responded with "considerable skepticism" towards the new plan.[308]

In an effort to bridge the differences between Europe and the U.S. (also in October 2004), the E3 came up with a new two-track approach that also found the endorsement of the European Union.[309] The new proposal combined incentives and disincentives for Iran and implied that Washington would join the talks at some point.[310] As Liberalism II helps to point out, this approach was conceptually similar to Condoleezza Rice's announcements from May 2006, which occurred 18 months later. Incentives for Iran included nuclear fuel supply from Russia and lifting the U.S. ban on exports of aircraft parts in return for a stop of Iranian enrichment activities.[311] The plan was discussed at a G8 meeting on the level of political directors in Washington on October 15.[312] As could be expected from the two liberal perspectives, John Bolton, who led the meeting with E3 officials, reacted with utter disdain towards the initiative and escaped any meaningful discussion of the plan.[313] When the E3 later inquired about the official American position, State Department spokesman Richard Boucher clarified that Washington had not "bought on, signed on or endorsed" the European proposal.[314] Washington agreed, however, to endorse the European-led effort to re-engage the Iranians.[315] As Liberalism II helps us understand, the efforts to impact U.S. Iran policy had no chance in succeeding.

Germany, France and the UK were forced to continue negotiations with Iran on their own, without the support for a coordinated approach from the Bush administration. The new agreement between the E3 and Iran, officially signed on November 15, committed Iran to a full suspension of all uranium enrichment-related and reprocessing activities while negotiations for a comprehensive

---

[308]   Ibid.

[309]   Silke Mertins and Hubert Wetzel, "EU bindet USA in Atomgespräche mit Iran ein," *Financial Times Deutschland*, 13 October 2004, 14, Steven R. Weisman, "U.S. in Talks With Europeans on a Nuclear Deal With Iran," *New York Times*, 12 October 2004, A12. Associated Press, "EU bereitet Angebot im Atomstreit mit Iran vor," *AP Worldstream - German*, 13 October 2004.

[310]   Mertins and Wetzel, "EU bindet USA in Atomgespräche mit Iran ein.", Weisman, "U.S. in Talks With Europeans on a Nuclear Deal With Iran." Associated Press, "EU bereitet Angebot im Atomstreit mit Iran vor."

[311]   Weisman, "Bush Confronts New Challenge On Issue of Iran." For the first time Germany considered punitive measures to be part of a package presented to Iran. Christian Wernicke, "Knüppel oder Karotte; Europa und Amerika wollen Iran mit "Zuckerbrot und Peitsche" von Atomplänen abbringen," *Süddeutsche Zeitung*, 15 October 2004, 6.

[312]   Weisman, "Bush Confronts New Challenge On Issue of Iran." For the first time Germany considered punitive measures to be part of a package presented to Iran. Wernicke, "Knüppel oder Karotte; Europa und Amerika wollen Iran mit "Zuckerbrot und Peitsche" von Atomplänen abbringen."

[313]   Steven R. Weisman, "U.S. Acquiesces in European Plan for Talks With Iran," *New York Times*, 16 October 2004, A7.

[314]   Guy Dinmore and Roula Khalaf, "US attacks European move on Iran Incentives Package," *Financial Times*, 21 October 2004, 9. Boucher specifically made it clear that Iran would not be supplied with civilian nuclear technology.

[315]   Robin Wright, "Europeans to Press Iran on Nuclear Plans; U.S. Backs Initiative Endorsed by G8 but Is Skeptical Tehran Will Honor Terms," *Washington Post*, 16 October 2004, A18.

long-term settlement between the EU and Iran would be under way.[316] Following its conclusion, the IAEA issued its most positive assessment in two years applauding Iran for its good cooperation.[317] Germany, however, continued to believe that U.S. involvement in the negotiation process of a final deal with Iran would be crucial to its success and that the possibility of the full normalization of relations between Washington and Tehran would be the "biggest carrot" that could be provided to Tehran.[318] Joschka Fischer stated that U.S. participation would give the negotiations a "considerable push."[319] Yet, as he also acknowledged, transatlantic policy coordination on the issue had been difficult despite his good personal relationship with Colin Powell. In his dealings with Powell, as Fischer admitted, he could never be sure if the Secretary of State represented the opinions of the whole Bush administration.[320]

3.3.   The Second Bush Administration (2005-2006)

The architecture of the second Bush administration gave America's European allies a chance to present new transatlantic policy recommendations on Iran to "bolster Atlanticists throughout the administration."[321] Shortly after his re-election, President Bush stated his intentions to visit Europe soon after his inauguration and to improve transatlantic ties.[322] Condoleezza Rice's nomination as Secretary of State was seen as sign for a fresh start in transatlantic relations in Germany.[323] As David Rothkopf observed, the fact that Rice surrounded herself with experienced traditionalists "signaled a desire to rebuild or restore relationships that were damaged because of the conduct of our invasion of Iraq."[324] While Condoleezza Rice avoided giving a clear indication on where the administration's Iran policy would be going during her Senate confirmation hearings, she quickly arranged an active exchange with the E3 in search for common transatlantic approaches towards

---

[316] Roger Howard, *EU3-Iran Deal Exposes Underlying International Tensions* Royal United Services Institute for Defence and Security Studies (RUSI), December 2004 [3 February 2006]; available from http://www.rusi.org/forward.php?structureID=S4058647E8B76D&ref=P41BD74CDB2209&showall=&print=true.

[317] Dafna Linzer, "U.N. Finds No Nuclear Bomb Program in Iran; Agency Report and Tehran's Deal With Europe Undercut Tougher U.S. Stance," *Washington Post*, 16 November 2004, A18.

[318] Steven R. Weisman, "U.S. and Europe Are at Odds, Again, This Time Over Iran," *New York Times*, 12 December 2004, A8.

[319] Christian Wernicke, "EU-Staaten hoffen auf US-Signal gegenüber Teheran," *Süddeutsche Zeitung*, 14 December 2004, 6.

[320] Roger Cohen, David E. Sanger, and Steven R. Weisman, "Challenging the Rest of the World With a New Order: The Bush Record - Fifth article in a series: Foreign Policy," *New York Times*, 12 October 2004, A1.

[321] Hulsman, "Bush's home run: neocon victory, realist world."

[322] Weisman, "Bush Confronts New Challenge On Issue of Iran." At this meeting Blair also tried to persuade Bush to support the European approach on Iran more comprehensively. Weisman, "Bush Confronts New Challenge On Issue of Iran."

[323] AP/dpa, "Schröder sieht Rice "durchaus gerne entgegen"," *Frankfurter Allgemeine Zeitung*, 18 November 2004, 1.

[324] Rothkopf, *Running the World* 437.

the nuclear crisis.[325] John Bolton, the major State Department representative in the way of a transatlantic approach, was not present at a secret meeting with European officials on Iran in January 2005 and he was subsequently kept out of U.S.-European coordination efforts.[326] As principal U.S. envoy on dealing with the E3, Under Secretary of State for Policy Nicholas Burns, played an increasingly central role in shaping U.S. diplomacy with Iran.[327] From a Liberalism II perspective, the personnel changes on the U.S. side were instrumental in enabling Germany to exert greater influence on American Iran policy. Germany took immediately advantage of the new situation in Washington. In late January 2005, Foreign Minister Fischer met with Condoleezza Rice to narrow transatlantic differences.[328] Early on in 2005, Rice realized that the U.S. would have to change its attitude with regard to the E3 negotiation process to counter the notion "that Europe was mediating between the United States and Iran."[329] Meanwhile, Chancellor Schröder urged the United States to actively support the E3 negotiations and to provide Iran not only with economic incentives but to take into account Iran's "legitimate security interests."[330] More overtly than before, Joschka Fischer also pushed for greater U.S. involvement, stating openly that "[i]f the United States were to engage positively […], it would substantially strengthen the European drive."[331] The public declaration of these urgings marked a new phase in German lobbying for U.S. support of multilateral diplomacy on Iran.

During his visit to Europe and Germany in February 2005, President Bush was impressed by Berlin's staunch opposition to Iran's nuclear ambitions and decided to consider some tactical changes in response.[332] Visiting Germany for the first time since the contested run-up to the Iraq War, Bush stated:

> "We spent time talking about Iran, and I want to thank Gerhard [Schröder] for taking the lead, along with Britain and France, on this important issue. It's vital that the Iranians hear the world speak with one voice that they shouldn't have a nuclear weapon. […] [D]iplomacy is just beginning. Iran is not Iraq. We've just started the diplomatic efforts, and I want to thank our friends for taking the lead and I will -- we will work with them to convince the mullahs that they

---

[325] Guy Dinmore, "No common ground with Iran, says Rice," *Financial Times (London)*, 20 January 2005, 8.

[326] Baker and Linzer, "Policy Shift Felt After Bolton's Departure From State Dept."

[327] Guy Dinmore and Daniel Dombey, "Moscow plays role in trying to resolve Iran nuclear dispute," *Financial Times (London)*, 20 May 2005, 9.

[328] Matthias Rüb, "Senat bestätigt die Ernennung von Condoleezza Rice," *Frankfurter Allgemeine Zeitung*, 27 January 2005, 4.

[329] Rice, "Rice optimistic about Bush's bold agenda in his second term, partial transcript of Secretary of State Condoleezza Rice's interview with editors and reporters."

[330] Gerhard Schröder, *Speech on the 41th Munich Conference on Security Policy* 12 February 2005 [14 May 2006]; available from http://www.securityconference.de.

[331] Richard Norton-Taylor, "US and Europe row over Iran," *The Guardian (London)*, 14 February 2005, 14.

[332] Wright, "Bush Weighs Offers to Iran; U.S. Might Join Effort to Halt Nuclear Program."

need to give up their nuclear ambitions."[333]

Bush's official endorsement of the E3 efforts at the summit with Chancellor Schröder in Mainz and Washington's following decision to provide spare U.S. aircraft part to Iran and drop the objection to its WTO membership was welcomed in Berlin and seen as increasing the chances of success for negotiations.[334] Following his trip to Europe, President Bush also changed his stance on the Russian proposal of providing nuclear fuel to Iran, something which Germany had been advocating for several months.[335] As a Liberalism II perspective goes to show, the President became crucially involved in deciding to support the E3 efforts. Even if the adjustments were limited in nature, Washington opened up to the ideas and policy proposals that the E3 favored (such as providing incentives and nuclear fuel to Iran). We may assume that these changes are related to the increased lobbying effort of Germany for more U.S. involvement. As U.S. administration hawks demanded, Germany, and its E3 partners agreed that if negotiations with Iran remained unsuccessful, the matter would have to be referred to the UN Security Council.[336]

Following these tactical changes, however, the E3 made only slow progress in their negotiations with Iran. After the conclusion of the 'Paris Agreement' in November 2004, German, French, and British envoys were meeting with Iranian counterparts on a monthly basis in Geneva to discuss a final settlement of the crisis in three working groups.[337] But the negotiations proceeded only slowly and the election of President Ahmadi-Nejad in June 2005 gave new urgency to coordinate Iran policy with the United States.[338] In early August, shortly before the E3 presented their final offer to Tehran, Nicholas Burns insisted on Iran to accept the proposal despite U.S. reservations regarding some details.[339] From a Liberalism II perspective, this display of flexibility can be attributed to the ongoing transatlantic coordination effort as well as the State Department's leadership on Iran policy. Tehran's rejection of the final E3 offer on August 7, 2005 and its decision to resume uranium conversion despite joint U.S.-European warnings—which effectively ended E3 negotiations with Tehran—prompted a new round of consultations between Washington and Europe.[340] During a visit to the United States, Chancellor Schröder demonstratively displayed his agreement with the

---

[333] The White House, *President Bush and Chancellor Schröder Discuss Partnership* 23 February 2005 [12 May 2006]; available from http://www.whitehouse.gov/news/releases/2005/02/print/20050223-4.html.

[334] Wright, "U.S., Allies May Have to Wait Out Iran's Presidential Vote."

[335] Weisman, "U.S. Reviewing European Proposal for Iran."

[336] Horst Bacia, "Neue Einigkeit über Ziel und Weg; Gegenüber Teheran arbeiten die Europäische Union und Washington jetzt zusammen," *Frankfurter Allgemeine Zeitung*, 14 March 2005, 6.

[337] Ibid.

[338] Wright, "U.S. and Europe Gird for Hard Line From Iran's President."

[339] Sonni Efron, "U.S. Urges Iran to Accept European Nuclear Offer," *Los Angeles Times*, 6 August 2005, A3.

[340] Linzer, "Iran Resumes Uranium Work, Ignores Warning."

U.S. President that an Iranian nuclear weapon was "unacceptable."[341] At the same time, however, Germany made sure that the door to future negotiations with Tehran remained open.[342] On September 15, 2005, three days before Germany's federal elections, the E3 foreign ministers met with the new Iranian President Ahmadi-Nejad and his envoy Ali Larijani (later to become the lead negotiator) at the sidelines of the United Nations annual summit in New York and restated their willingness to continue negotiations.[343]

After the September 18 federal elections, a new German government under Chancellor Angela Merkel and Foreign Minister Frank-Walter Steinmeier continued German Iran policy where Schröder and Fischer had left off. Germany's coordination efforts with Washington and its influence, however, was about to intensify. On November 30, 2005, Foreign Minister Steinmeier met with Condoleezza Rice, Robert Zoellick and Stephen Hadley in Washington.[344] Rice as well as Zoellick paid immediate return visits to Berlin during the following days.[345]

In January 2006, the breaking of IAEA seals at the Natanz enrichment facility by Iran diminished Berlin's hopes for a continuation of negotiations. At a meeting in Berlin on January 12, Frank-Walter Steinmeier declared that European diplomacy with Iran had reached a "dead end" and that the E3 had agreed to involve the UN Security Council involvement to enforce IAEA resolutions.[346] Germany still looked for ways to solve the issue in a multilateral setting, but the E3 also came to the conclusion that any new round of diplomacy would demand a greater active involvement of other major powers.[347] Washington was seen as the crucial partner to keep diplomacy with regard to Iran alive, but progress also depended on Russian and Chinese support.[348] Berlin focused on establishing support for a multilateral approach in close coordination based on unity between these major

---

[341] Rudolph Chimelli, "Wahl in Iran beunruhigt den Westen," *Süddeutsche Zeitung*, 27 June 2005, 1, Anne E. Kornblut, "Bush Hears Endorsement From Schroder About Iran," *New York Times*, 28 June 2005, A12. Later, in August 2005, Schröder flirted with using the issue of Iran for his re-election campaign. See: Peter Dausend and Nikolaus Blome, "Schröder zieht Iran-Konflikt in den Wahlkampf," *Die Welt*, 15 August 2005.

[342] Christopher Adams, Najmeh Bozorgmehr, and Guy Dinmore, "Iran defies warning on uranium activity," *Financial Times (London)*, 9 August 2005, 7, Louis Charbonneau, "EU wants UN to take up Iran nuclear issue - Germany," *Reuters*, 7 September 2005, Linzer, "Bush Cautiously Optimistic as Iran Offers to Negotiate."

[343] dpa, "EU three meet with Iran on nuclear programme, no progress seen," *Deutsche Presse-Agentur*, 15 September 2005, Matthias Rüb, "Fischer bekräftigt Forderung nach Sitz im Sicherheitsrat; Abschluß des UN-Gipfels in New York; Treffen der EU-3 mit iranischem Präsidenten," *Frankfurter Allgemeine Zeitung*, 17 September 2005, 1.

[344] Nico Fried, "Zum Auftakt viel guter Wille; Berlin und Washington suchen Gemeinsamkeiten," *Süddeutsche Zeitung*, 1 December 2005, 6.

[345] Ibid.

[346] Auswärtiges Amt, *Presseerklärungen der E3 Außenminister und des Hohen Repräsentanten der EU in Berlin zum Iran* 12 January 2006 [12 June 2006]; available from http://www.auswaertiges-amt.de/diplo/de/Infoservice/Presse/Meldungen/2006/01-03/060112-E3ZumIran.html.

[347] Johannes Leithäuser, "Die EU will den Iran-Konflikt in den Sicherheitsrat bringen," *Frankfurter Allgemeine Zeitung*, 13 January 2006, 1.

[348] Ralf Beste, Ralf Neukirch, and Gabor Steingart, "Der dritte Weg," *Der Spiegel* 23 Januar 2006.

powers.[349]

During Angela Merkel's inaugural visit to Washington, President Bush and the Chancellor quickly established a good personal relationship and agreed on a closely coordinated approach towards Iran.[350] Merkel's first visit to Moscow—although less amicable—similarly resulted in an agreement with Russia to coordinate Iran policy more closely.[351] On January 30, after Germany's lobbying efforts, the E3 foreign ministers met with their counterparts from Russia, China, and the United States (E3+3) in London.[352] The group agreed on reporting Iran to the UN Security Council through the IAEA in February, but it remained split on how to proceed from there.[353] By referring Iran to the UN, Berlin sought to underline the IAEA's demand for the suspension of uranium enrichment while avoiding an escalation of the crisis.[354]

Although holding no seat on the UN Security Council, Germany remained an important player in the diplomatic process as part of the E3 and was invited to participate in UN negotiations.[355] During the following months, Berlin pursued two strategies that both aimed at involving Washington more actively. The first drew on Germany's earlier idea to develop a carrot-and-stick approach. It evolved from a close coordination effort between the political directors of the E3 foreign ministries and the State Department.[356] Michael Schäfer from Germany, Stanislas de Laboulaye from France, John Sawyers from the UK, and Robert Cooper, an aide to Javier Solana at the EU council had been working closely with Nicholas Burns on Iran.[357] By March 2006, this group realized that Russia and China would not accept "significant sanctions over the coming months, certainly not without further efforts to bring the Iranians around."[358] To get Russian and Chinese support for a chapter VII UN Security Council resolution (which would lay the foundations for sanctions) the diplomats agreed to present another package of incentives to Iran which "ideally [...] would have the explicit backing of Russia, China and the United States as well as

---

[349]   Ibid.

[350]   Paul Richter, "Bush, Merkel United On Iran," *Los Angeles Times*, 14 January 2006, Alexander Skiba and Stephen F. Szabo, "Merkel in Washington, Part Deux," *AICGS Advisor*, no. 28 April (2006).

[351]   DW, *Merkel und Putin einig gegen Teheran* 17 January 2006 [12 June 2006]; available from http://www.welt.de/data/2006/01/17/832604.html.

[352]   Kessler, "Iran Warned, but Russia, China Dissent on Action."

[353]   Ibid.

[354]   Oliver Thränert, "Iran Before the Security Council? German Perspectives and Goals," in *SWP Comments* (Stiftung Wissenschaft und Politik, 2006). As Chancellor Merkel had indicated to President Bush in January 2006, Berlin was supportive of "smart sanctions" against Iran but preferred to impose these sanctions through the United Nations. Guy Dinmore, "US allies urge direct dialogue with Iran," *Financial Times (London)*, 3 May 2006, 8.

[355]   ap, "Diplomaten der ständigen Sicherheitsratsmitglieder beraten über Iran; Auch Deutschland zu Gesprächen am Montag eingeladen," *Associated Press Worldstream - German*, 16 March 2006.

[356]   Times Online, *Leaked letter in full: UK diplomat outlines Iran strategy.*

[357]   Ibid.

[358]   Ibid.

the E3."[359] Berlin was convinced that Russian and Chinese support was essential in any new round of talks, but that U.S. support and eventual direct involvement was a *conditio sine qua non*.[360] Liberalism II allows appreciating the subtlety as well as the importance of this transatlantic coordination effort at the political director's level. Nicholas Burns emerges as an important individual who may have shaped the adjustments of U.S. Iran policy in May 2006 to a great extent. He also appears to have been amenable to E3 ideas about how to proceed on Iran.

Another German strategy was to urge Washington to hold bilateral talks with Iran.[361] During his visit to Washington on April 4, Frank-Walter Steinmeier urged U.S. National Security Advisor Stephen Hadley to engage Iran directly and Chancellor Merkel raised the issue repeatedly with President Bush.[362] At the core of both strategies was the assumption that Iran had legitimate security concerns that only the U.S. could address.[363]

During her second visit to Washington since taking office, Merkel again emphasized that Germany preferred a united step-by-step approach.[364] As the Liberalism II perspective helps to show, the German Chancellor, due to her amicable relationship with President Bush, played an increasingly vital role with regard to determining policy and coordinating the transatlantic approach towards Iran. During the critical phases of presidential decision making in the White House, Merkel remained closely in touch with President Bush.[365]

3.4.   Summary

The Liberalism II perspective shifts the focus towards Germany's policy on Iran and its desire for greater U.S. involvement in the E3 negotiation effort. As could be expected on the basis of the findings of the Liberalism I perspective, Germany had little influence on U.S. Iran policy during the first Bush administration. But unlike Liberalism I suggests, this was not only due to Colin Powell's weak institutional position inside the Bush administration and John Bolton's campaign against U.S.

---

[359] Ibid.
[360] Guy Dinmore, Demetri Sevastopulo, and Hubert Wetzel, "Germany urges US to hold talks with Iran," *Financial Times (London)*, 5 April 2006, 5, Hubert Wetzel, "Europa drängt USA zu Dialog mit Iran; Im Atomstreit könnte Washington ausreichende Sicherheitsgarantien bieten," *Financial Times Deutschland*, 5 April 2006, 15.
[361] Dinmore, Sevastopulo, and Wetzel, "Germany urges US to hold talks with Iran.", Wetzel, "Europa drängt USA zu Dialog mit Iran; Im Atomstreit könnte Washington ausreichende Sicherheitsgarantien bieten." See also: Dinmore, "US allies urge direct dialogue with Iran."
[362] Welt.de, *Steinmeier drängt USA zu direkten Gesprächen mit Teheran* Die Welt, 4 April 2006 [12 June 2006]; available from http://www.welt.de/data/2006/04/04/869750.html.
[363] Martin Winter, "Die Koalition der Unsicheren," *Süddeutsche Zeitung*, 22 April 2006, 9.
[364] Günther Bannas, "Bush und Merkel wollen Iran mit Eintracht und Diplomatie zusetzen," *Frankfurter Allgemeine Zeitung*, 5 May 2006, 1.
[365] Cooper and Sanger, "A talk at lunch that shifted the stance on Iran."

support for the E3. Inherent in the 'Tehran Declaration' negotiated by the E3 in 2003, was the premise that Iran would not be referred to the UN Security Council. As long as Tehran was able to divide the E3 from the United States on the course of multilateral diplomacy, Germany's potential impact on U.S. Iran policy remained severely limited. The make-up of the second Bush administration provided fertile ground for greater German was influence. Transatlantic policy coordination was additionally facilitated by Iran's continuously defiant behavior. Under the direction of Condoleezza Rice, the State Department demonstrated a greater willingness to take into consideration European concerns and policy proposals. In this regard, John Bolton's removal from active U.S. nonproliferation and the arrival of a committed Atlanticist—Nicholas Burns—who took the lead on Iran was of central importance.[366] Liberalism II suggests that Germany was instrumental in winning President Bush's approval of and support for the E3 efforts in February 2005. The perspective also suggests that the new government of Angela Merkel and Frank-Walter Steinmeier had an even greater impact on U.S. Iran policy. Merkel appeared to be especially successful in keeping President Bush committed to multilateral diplomacy on Iran.[367]

---

[366] Efron, "Harsh Critic of U.N. Named Ambassador."

[367] Ralf Beste et al., "Offerte aus dem Weißen Haus," *Der Spiegel* 3 June 2006. See also: Peter Baker, Dafna Linzer, and Thomas E. Ricks, "U.S. Is Studying Military Strike Options on Iran," *Washington Post*, 9 April 2006, A01.

C.   Conclusion and Outlook

1.   Solving the Empirical Puzzle

The theoretical perspectives have shown distinct merits when it comes to explaining and contextualizing the adjustments of U.S. Iran policy and growing transatlantic policy coordination. Like a flashlight in the dark, the theories focus the analyst's attention on different independent variables affecting American foreign policy.

Let us recall the three hypotheses from the outset of our analysis. The neorealist perspective stipulated that a decline of U.S. power limited Washington's freedom of action in the realm of foreign policy and forced it to seek the support of its allies to counter Iran's nuclear ambitions. The first liberal approach (Liberalism I) led us to expect that changes within the make-up of the Bush administration caused policy adjustments during the second term (2005/2006). The second liberal perspective (Liberalism II) drew our attention to the influence of Germany, stipulating that Berlin's growing influence during the second Bush administration co-determined the changes of U.S. Iran policy.

The neorealist perspective is successful in highlighting the larger context and emphasizes the constraints under which U.S. foreign policy had to be formulated and implemented. As the analysis shows, declining military or economic power cannot be identified as the key independent variable shaping America's approach towards Iran. It is primarily America's waning political influence, following the invasion of Iraq, which put severe limits on the usefulness of U.S. "hard power." Decreasing "soft power" made U.S. global leadership on Iran exceedingly difficult and forced it to rely on European-led multilateral diplomacy.[368] Additionally, Iran's emergence as an assertive regional power—especially after the election of President Ahmadi-Nejad in June 2005—acting in defiance of the international community, facilitated greater transatlantic policy coordination.[369] The

---

[368]   Cf. Eberhard Sandschneider, "Die USA als dominierende Weltmacht," in *Jahrbuch Internationale Politik 2003/2004*, ed. Helmut Hubel, et al., *Jahrbücher des Forschungsinstituts der Deutschen Gesellschaft für Auswärtige Politik* (München: R. Oldenbourg Verlag, 2005), 10.

[369]   The facilitating impact of Iran's defiant behavior is also recognized by the liberal approaches.

neorealist perspective has limitations, however, when it comes to explaining why U.S. policy adjustments occurred only after President Bush's re-election in November 2004. The perspective also remains indifferent to the multiplicity of domestic constraints, under which U.S. foreign policy had to be formulated. The neorealist billiard ball model of international relations suppresses a nuanced view of how U.S. Iran policy was forged between 2003 and 2006.

In this regard, Liberalism I is well suited to complement the neorealism's point of view. It draws the analysts' attention to the poly-archic nature of the Bush administration during the first term and highlights the concentration of presidential power in the second cabinet. While the State Department was rivaled and constrained by the Pentagon and the Vice President's Office in 2003 and 2004, this unproductive internal gridlock was eased in 2005 and 2006. President Bush re-established an efficient working relationship between the White House and the State Department by promoting a trusted friend, Condoleezza Rice, as Secretary of State.

The liberal perspective also highlights that traces of two contradictory themes can be found in U.S. Iran policy since 2005, reflecting the personal preferences of the President and a crude interim compromise between the most powerful individuals within his cabinet. In terms of means, the second Bush administration gave priority to multilateral diplomacy in coordination with the E3, China and Russia. It committed itself to supporting the European approach and to participate in potential negotiations with Iran. America's missionary zeal of spreading freedom and democracy, however, remained on the front burner nonetheless. As the National Security Strategy (NSS) of March 2006 unambiguously stated, the ultimate goal of U.S. Iran policy is to "bring freedom to the Iranian people" and to "block the threats posed by the regime while expanding our engagement and outreach to the people the regime is oppressing."[370] Liberalism I is well suited to explain the internal dynamics of the Bush administration and to highlight that U.S. Iran policy flowed from a hard-fought bureaucratic compromise that remained ultimately at odds with the E3 engagement approach. Liberalism I has deficiencies, however, when it comes to pointing out and explaining the fine print of the policy adjustments.

The perspective of Liberalism II helps to close this gap partially. It allows us to look at U.S. Iran policy from a transatlantic angle. The perspective highlights how Germany has worked to constrain and influence American policy on Iran. The second liberal perspective shows that Berlin realized that transatlantic policy coordination was crucial to securing a deal with Iran on the nuclear issue after Iran had abrogated the 'Tehran Declaration' of October 2003 in early 2004. Iran's more assertive stance helped to facilitate greater transatlantic unity. Berlin partially succeeded in

---

[370]   The White House, *The National Security Strategy of the United States of America* (Washington, D.C.: March 2006) 20.

promoting the concept of combining diplomatic pressure with tangible economic, political, and security-related incentives to induce Iran to give up its suspicious nuclear activities in Washington. Due to a lack of empirical data and the possible influence of other variables, evaluating Germany's exact impact on the formulation of U.S. policy must remain vague. Liberalism II, however, enables us to point out the importance of President Bush's visit to Europe in February 2005 and Nicholas Burns' meetings with E3 his colleagues in early 2006. It also allows us to underscore that German-American policy coordination has improved and intensified after the election of Chancellor Merkel in the fall of 2005. Frau Merkel has used her good personal relationship with President Bush to push for greater transatlantic coordination on Iran.

At the outset of this book, I asked the following question: **Why has American Iran policy shifted towards supporting the European approach between 2003 and 2006?** As the analysis has shown, Washington was unable to formulate an autonomous policy according to its original preferences of sanctioning and isolating Iran when the nuclear program emerged as pressing security challenge at the beginning of 2003. Faced with a lack of good military options and a rapid decline of political influence around the world, the United States was forced to reconsider its approach. While a dysfunctional national security policy team prohibited a policy shift in favor of multilateral diplomacy during President Bush's first term, personnel changes in the second administration paved the way for gradual adjustments. A combination of three factors can be made accountable for the policy changes in 2005 and 2006: First, America's ability to act in accord with its original preferences—i.e. unilaterally—was severely limited. Second, the streamlining of President Bush's foreign policy staff after his re-election in November 2004 facilitated greater transatlantic policy coordination by strengthening the internationalist wing within the Bush administration. Third, Germany's influence on the process of formulating U.S. Iran policy grew during the second Bush administration and helped to reshape Washington's position in favor of multilateral negotiations with Iran.

Some critical remarks are in order as well. Although the three theoretical perspectives carry the seeds of complementarity, none of them is able to explain the issue of adjusting U.S. Iran policy in a satisfying way on its own. This lack of explanatory power hints at the deficiencies of IR theory when it comes to informing actual and current decision-making of policy practitioners. It would be a great leap forward for the discipline of International Relations and foreign policy analysis if it were possible to devise a new theoretical approach that successfully combines taking into account the structural constraints that states are faced with (by clearly conceptualizing what constitutes a state's power position) as well as the domestic and transnational aspects of foreign policy.

2.   Iran and Future Transatlantic Policy Coordination

Empirically, the shifts of 2005 and 2006 mark a new chapter in U.S. Iran policy. Yet—in light of the thorough analysis of this book—important qualifications are in order. Washington's reversal of previous positions was achieved only after "a good bit of bureaucratic blood [had been] spilled."[371] Due to its nature as a trade-off between different key players inside the Bush administration, the new policy can hardly be regarded as a glaring success for proponents of engagement, multilateral diplomacy and transatlantic policy coordination. It is only a tentative step in that direction and remains entirely reversible.

What lessons for transatlantic policy coordination can be drawn from the case of Iran's nuclear program? As Stephen Szabo cautioned in the introductory quote, "[t]he key question for the future is whether the common strategic interests that remain can be shaped to give the relationship a realistic basis."[372] Judged by the analysis of this book, it can hardly be said that Iran has emerged as a new common strategic interest for both sides of the Atlantic. However, as developments of recent years show, important players in the Bush administration have opened up to the idea of multilateral diplomacy on Iran (and elsewhere—such as North Korea). To maintain the fragile transatlantic coalition on Iran that has developed since 2005, the United States must continue to listen to European concerns, while Europe must remain a serious partner in confronting Tehran.

Germany's lobbying for greater active U.S. involvement is bound to continue, should Iran refuse to come to the negotiating table, as seems all too likely.[373] Berlin is well-advised to track the internal fault lines within the Bush administration closely and continue to leverage Washington by targeting senior State Department officials and President Bush directly with practical policy proposals. In order to increase the persuasiveness of its arguments in Washington, Germany will have to show flexibility when it comes to implementing (smart) sanctions against Iran.[374] A particular obstacle to greater U.S. involvement in diplomacy with Tehran is the all-pervasive ideology of "democratism" in the elite circles of Washington's policy makers.[375] The promotion of democracy in Iran (and other countries) remains a widely shared goal within the Bush administration. A fluffy and utterly

---

[371] Sick, "The US Offer to Iran."

[372] Szabo, *Parting Ways* 140.

[373] IRNA, *Iran rejects preconditions for nuclear talks* 20 August 2006 [12 September 2006]; available from
        http://www.irna.ir/en/news/view/line-24/0608201710152643.htm.

[374] Guy Dinmore, "White House reverts to cold war containment," *Financial Times (London)*, 12 October 2006.

[375] Cf. Anatol Lieven and John Hulsman, *The Folly Of Exporting Democracy* TomPaine.com, 12 September 2006 [13 September 2006];
        available from http://www.tompaine.com/articles/2006/09/12/the_folly_of_exporting_democracy.php.

idealistic concept, the notion exporting western-style democracy runs contrary to a serious dialogue between Washington and Tehran. The fact that—to a varying degree—this idea has found the support from President Bush, Condoleezza Rice as well as from Vice President Cheney should make Germany and other countries suspicious of Washington's future intentions towards Iran. As the President declared just shortly before he approved of the Rice plan to support the E3 in late May 2006 at the West Point military academy:

> "The message has spread from Damascus to Tehran that the future belongs to freedom–and we
> will not rest until the promise of liberty reaches every people and every nation."[376]

Unfortunately, from a European point of view, the belief that democracy will work as a panacea to all the world's ills is shared by a many in the leaderships of Democrats and Republicans alike.[377] The "democratist" ideology may therefore present a great obstacle to coordinated transatlantic policies in the future.

Should multilateral diplomacy with Iran fail, President Bush, who reportedly sees Iran "as a serious menace that must be dealt with before his presidency ends," will be tempted to resort to other means.[378] Despite a lack of good military options, Washington might conclude that "[t]here is only one thing worse than the United States exercising a military option, and that is a nuclear-armed Iran."[379] In order to avoid these two pitfalls for transatlantic policy coordination—a more dominant role for the ideology of aggressive democracy promotion as well as a military 'solution' to Iran's nuclear program—Germany must continue to build a critical mass with other countries to keep the diplomatic option alive and continue to promote direct talks between Washington and Tehran. The menace from Iran's nuclear program (and the continuing violence in Iraq) will only be stopped if Washington acknowledges that all regional players, including Tehran, have legitimate national interests that cannot be ignored.

Berlin, October 2006

---

[376] The White House, *President Delivers Commencement Address at the United States Military Academy at West Point, Mitchie Stadium, United States Military Academy at West Point* 27 May 2006 [5 June 2006]; available from http://www.whitehouse.gov/news/releases/2006/05/20060527-1.html. (emphasis added)

[377] Anatol Lieven and John Hulsman, *Ethical Realism: A Vision for America's Role in the World* (New York: Pantheon, 2006) 4.

[378] Baker, Linzer, and Ricks, "U.S. Is Studying Military Strike Options on Iran."

[379] Senator John McCain in: CBS News, *CBS News' Face the Nation* 15 January 2006 available from www.cbsnews.com/htdocs/pdf/face_011506.pdf.

Bibliography

Adams, Christopher, Najmeh Bozorgmehr, and Guy Dinmore. "Iran defies warning on uranium activity." *Financial Times (London)* 9 August 2005, 7.

Allen, Mike. "Iran 'Will Be Dealt With,' Bush says; Bid to Start at UN, President Says." *Washington Post* 22 April 2004, A06.

———. "Powell Announced his Resignation; Secretary of State Clashed With Cheney and Rumsfeld; Rice to Succeed Him." *Washington Post* 16 November 2004, A01.

Allison, Graham T., and Philip D. Zelikow. *Essence of Decision. Explaining the Cuban Missile Crisis.* 2nd ed., New York: Longman, 1999.

Anderson, John Ward, and Glenn Kessler. "U.N. Nuclear Agency Reports Iran to Security Council." *Washington Post* 4 February 2006.

ap. "Diplomaten der ständigen Sicherheitsratsmitglieder beraten über Iran; Auch Deutschland zu Gesprächen am Montag eingeladen." *Associated Press Worldstream - German* 16 March 2006.

AP/dpa. "Schröder sieht Rice "durchaus gerne entgegen"." *Frankfurter Allgemeine Zeitung* 18 November 2004, 1.

Armitage, Richard L. U.S. Policy and Iran. Testimony before the Senate Foreign Relations Committee 28 October 2003 [acessed: 4 April 2005]. Available from http://www.state.gov/s/d/former/armitage/remarks/25682.htm.

Associated Press. "EU bereitet Angebot im Atomstreit mit Iran vor." *AP Worldstream - German* 13 October 2004.

———. "Iran fordert Zugang zu waffenfähiger Atomtechnologie - "Wunschliste" an EU-Staaten." *AP Worldstream - German* 9 August 2004.

Auswärtiges Amt. "Der Nahe und Mittlere Osten - Überlegungen aus europäischer Sicht" - Rede von Bundesaußenminister Fischer auf der Herzliya Konferenz 12 December 2003 [acessed: 5 May 2006]. Available from http://www.auswaertiges-amt.de/diplo/de/Infoservice/Presse/Reden/2003/031217-FischerNaherMittlererOsten.html.

———. Interview mit Bundesaußenminister Fischer zu verschiedenen außenpolitischen Themen in der "Stuttgarter Zeitung"(Auszug) 27 October 2003 [acessed: 7 May 2006]. Available from http://www.auswaertiges-amt.de/diplo/de/Infoservice/Presse/Interviews/2003/031027-StuttgarterZeitung,templateId=html.html.

———. "Notfalls muss in der EU eine Gruppe vorangehen" - Interview von Bundesaußenminister Fischer zur gemeinsamen europäischen Außen- und Sicherheitspolitik im Handelsblatt 3 April 2003 [acessed: 7 May 2006]. Available from http://www.auswaertiges-amt.de/diplo/de/Infoservice/Presse/Interviews/2003/030403-Handelsblatt,templateId=html.html.

————. Presseerklärungen der E3 Außenminister und des Hohen Repräsentanten der EU in Berlin zum Iran 12 January 2006 [acessed: 12 June 2006]. Available from http://www.auswaertiges-amt.de/diplo/de/Infoservice/Presse/Meldungen/2006/01-03/060112-E3ZumIran.html.

Bacia, Horst. "Außenminister uneinig über Vorgehen gegen Iran; Fischer: Kann Fall für den Sicherheitsrat werden." *Frankfurter Allgemeine Zeitung* 6 September 2004, 8.

————. "Neue Einigkeit über Ziel und Weg; Gegenüber Teheran arbeiten die Europäische Union und Washington jetzt zusammen." *Frankfurter Allgemeine Zeitung* 14 March 2005, 6.

Baker, Peter. "The Security Adviser Who Wants the Role, Not the Stage." 29 January 2006, A04.

Baker, Peter, and Dafna Linzer. "Policy Shift Felt After Bolton's Departure From State Dept." *Washington Post* 20 June 2005, A02.

Baker, Peter, Dafna Linzer, and Thomas E. Ricks. "U.S. Is Studying Military Strike Options on Iran." *Washington Post* 9 April 2006, A01.

Bannas, Günther. "Bush und Merkel wollen Iran mit Eintracht und Diplomatie zusetzen." *Frankfurter Allgemeine Zeitung* 5 May 2006, 1.

Baumann, Rainer, Volker Rittberger, and Wolfgang Wagner. "Neorealist foreign policy theory." In: German foreign policy since unification. Theories and Case Studies, edited by Volker Rittberger, Manchester: Manchester University Press, 2001: 37-67.

Behrendt, Sven. "Reintegration und Prävention von „Risikostaaten"." *Internationale Politik,* 6 (1999): 29-34.

Belasco, Amy. "The Cost of Iraq, Afghanistan, and Other Global War on Terror Operations Since 9/11." Congressional Research Service, 2006.

Berman, Ilan. *Tehran Rising: Iran's Challenge to the United States,* Lanham: Rowman & Littlefield, 2006.

Beste, Ralf, Hans Hoyng, Georg Mascolo, and Ralf Neukirch. "Offerte aus dem Weißen Haus." *Der Spiegel* 3 June 2006, 22-26.

Beste, Ralf, Ralf Neukirch, and Gabor Steingart. "Der dritte Weg." *Der Spiegel* 23 Januar 2006, 22.

Binyon, Michael, and Bronwen Maddox. "US sets sights on toppling Iran regime." *The Times of London* 17 July 2004.

Blitz, James, and Guy Dinmore. "Rice fails to win support for Iran referral to Security Council." *Financial Times (London)* 17 October 2005, 12.

Bokhari, Kamran. The Nuclear Deadlines and a Strengthening Iran 22 August 2006 [acessed: 24 August 2006]. Available from http://www.stratfor.com/.

Borger, Julian, and Ewen MacAskill. "U-turn by White House as it blocks direct talks with Iran." *The Guardian (London)* 25 May 2006.

Branigin, William. "Bush, Schroeder Oppose Iran's Nuclear Ambitions." *Washington Post,* 23 February 2005.

Brooks, Peter. Nuclear Wal-Mart *The Heritage Foundation,* February 2004 [acessed: 17 May 2006]. Available from http://www.heritage.org/Press/Commentary/ed020904a.cfm.

Busby, Joshua William. Veto Powers and Political Distance in the Western Alliance 2004 [acessed: 12 June 2006]. Available from wws.princeton.edu/jbusby/papers/apsa2004.pdf.

Busse, Nikolas. "Beratungen über Iran-Resolution; Widerstand gegen europäisch-amerikanischen Entwurf." *Frankfurter Allgemeine Zeitung* 12 March 2004, 8.

————. "Berlin abwartend im Atomstreit mit Iran." *Frankfurter Allgemeine Zeitung* 3 August 2004, 4.

CATO Institute. Ethical Realism: A Vision for America's Role in the World, A Cato Institute Book Forum featuring the authors Anatol Lieven, New America Foundation; John Hulsman, German Council on Foreign Relations; with comments by Lawrence Kaplan, The New Republic; and Joseph Cirincione, Center for American Progress. 10 October 2006 [acessed: 13 October 2006]. Available from http://www.cato.org/event.php?eventid=3227.

CBS News. CBS News' Face the Nation 15 January 2006 [acessed. Available from www.cbsnews.com/htdocs/pdf/face_011506.pdf.

Charbonneau, Louis. "EU wants UN to take up Iran nuclear issue - Germany." *Reuters* 7 September 2005.

Chimelli, Rudolph. "Neue Gespräche über Irans Atomprogramm." *Süddeutsche Zeitung* 29. July 2004, 8.

————. "Wahl in Iran beunruhigt den Westen." *Süddeutsche Zeitung* 27 June 2005, 1.

Christian Science Monitor. Neoconservatives and their blueprint for US power: Key figures *CSM,* [acessed: 12 June 2006]. Available from http://www.csmonitor.com/specials/neocon/index.html.

CIA. The World Factbook: United States *Central Intelligence Agency,* 2006 [acessed: 12 September 2006]. Available from https://www.cia.gov/cia/publications/factbook/geos/us.html#Econ.

CNN.com. Commander in Chief lands on USS Lincoln 2 May 2003 [acessed: 12 February 2006]. Available from http://www.cnn.com/2003/ALLPOLITICS/05/01/bush.carrier.landing/.

Cohen, Roger, David E. Sanger, and Steven R. Weisman. "Challenging the Rest of the World With a New Order: The Bush Record - Fifth article in a series: Foreign Policy." *New York Times* 12 October 2004, A1.

Cooper, Helene, and David E. Sanger. "A talk at lunch that shifted the stance on Iran." 4 June 2006, A08.

Council on Foreign Relations. Interview with Flynt Leverett: Bush Administration 'Not Serious' About Dealing With Iran 31 March 2006 [acessed: 13 June 2006]. Available from http://www.cfr.org/publication/10326/.

Daase, Christopher, Susanne Feske, and Ingo Peters, eds. *Internationale Risikopolitik. Der Umgang mit neuen Gefahren in den internationalen Beziehungen.* Baden Baden: Nomos, 2002.

Daniel, Caroline, and Guy Dinmore. Pentagon loses responsibility for rebuilding Iraq 15 December 2005 [acessed: 12 June 2006]. Available from http://www.ft.com/cms/s/4f826e9e-6d0f-11da-90c2-0000779e2340.html.

Dausend, Peter, and Nikolaus Blome. "Schröder zieht Iran-Konflikt in den Wahlkampf." *Die Welt* 15 August 2005.

Dempsey, Judy. "Brussel urges Iran to reform or face bar on trade talks revival." *Financial Times (London)* 4 May 2004, 9.

DeYoung, Karen, and Glenn Kessler. "Foreign Policy: After Iraq, U.S. Debates The Next Steps." *Washington Post* 13 April 2003, A01.

Dinmore, Guy. "Europeans urge Bush to adopt Kerry's line on Iran." *Financial Times (London)* 2 October 2004, 6.

———. "Hawks and pragmatists to mix on Rice's team." *Financial Times (London)* 17 January 2005, 8.

———. "Iran ready for high-level talks, US resists." *Financial Times (London)* 7 April 2006.

———. "No common ground with Iran, says Rice." *Financial Times (London)* 20 January 2005, 8.

———. "Presidential rivals take divergent views on Tehran 'atomic threat': Bush is for isolation while Kerry wants to talk." *Financial Times (London)* 2 September 2004, 7.

———. "US allies urge direct dialogue with Iran." *Financial Times (London)* 3 May 2006, 8.

———. "US debates military strikes on 'nuclear Iran'." *Financial Times (London)* 16 September 2004, 12.

———. "US split over Iranian bid to renew relations." *Financial Times (London)* 17 March 2004, 1.

———. "White House reverts to cold war containment." *Financial Times (London)* 12 October 2006.

Dinmore, Guy, and Daniel Dombey. "Moscow plays role in trying to resolve Iran nuclear dispute." *Financial Times (London)* 20 May 2005, 9.

———. Washington 'hawks' oppose EU3 plan for Iran *Financial Times (London)*, 23 May 2006 [acessed: 23 May 2006]. Available from http://news.ft.com/cms/s/f5f3b27c-ea7f-11da-9566-0000779e2340.html.

Dinmore, Guy, Carola Hoyos, and Gareth Smyth. "US casts doubt on new leader's legitimacy." *Financial Times (London)* 27 June 2005, 5.

Dinmore, Guy, and Roula Khalaf. "US attacks European move on Iran Incentives Package." *Financial Times* 21 October 2004, 9.

Dinmore, Guy, Demetri Sevastopulo, and Hubert Wetzel. "Germany urges US to hold talks with Iran." *Financial Times (London)* 5 April 2006, 5.

Dinmore, Guy, and Gareth Smyth. "Support grows for UN showdown with Iran over nuclear programme." *Financial Times (London)* 5 August 2004, 9.

———. "US and UK develop democracy strategy for Iran." *Financial Times (London)* 22 April 2006, 9.

Dinmore, Guy, and Hubert Wetzel. "President faces hard sell over Iran policy." *Financial Times (London)* 25 February 2005, 8.

dpa. "EU three meet with Iran on nuclear programme, no progress seen." *Deutsche Presse-Agentur* 15 September 2005.

dpa/Reuters. "Iran kündigt Atomabkommen mit Europäern." *Süddeutsche Zeitung* 2 August 2004, 6.

DW. Merkel und Putin einig gegen Teheran 17 January 2006 [acessed: 12 June 2006]. Available from http://www.welt.de/data/2006/01/17/832604.html.

Economist, The. Iran, Libya and nukes 13 March 2004 [acessed: 12 May 2006]. Available from http://www.economist.com/world/africa/displaystory.cfm?story_id=E1_NVDPDGN.

Efron, Sonni. "Bush Softens Stance on Iran." *Los Angeles Times* 12 March 2005, A1.

————. "Harsh Critic of U.N. Named Ambassador." *Los Angeles Times* 8 March 2005, A1.

————. "U.S. Options Few in Feud With Iran; Alarmed at Tehran's nuclear ambitions, Washington for now can only watch and wait." *Los Angeles Times* 13 December 2004, A1.

————. "U.S. Urges Iran to Accept European Nuclear Offer." *Los Angeles Times* 6 August 2005, A3.

Efron, Sonni, and Mark Mazzetti. "U.S. May Aid Iran Activists." *Los Angeles Times* 4 March 2004, A1.

Fallows, James. "Will Iran be Next? Soldiers, Spies, and Diplomats Conduct a Classic Pentagon Wargame-With Sobering Results." *The Atlantic Monthly* December 2004, 99-110.

FAS. "Auswärtiges Amt: Teheran will sich Atomwaffen beschaffen." *Frankfurter Allgemeine Sonntagszeitung* 22 June 2003, 2.

Fischer, Joschka. "Die Rekonstruktion des Westens. Außenminister Fischer über Europa, Amerika und die gemeinsamen strategischen Aufgaben." *Frankfurter Allgemeine Zeitung* 6 March 2004, 9.

————. Europe and the Future of the Transatlantic Relations, Speech at Princeton University *Germany.info*, 20 November 2003 [acessed: 13 May 2005]. Available from http://germany.info/relaunch/politics/speeches/112003.html.

Fletcher, Michael A., and Keith B. Richburg. "Bush Tries to Allay E.U. Worry Over Iran; Notion of U.S. Attack 'Is Simply Ridiculous'." *Washington Post* 23 February 2005, A01.

FOXNews.com. House Majority Whip Backs Iraq Action 22 August 2002 [acessed: 13 July 2006]. Available from www.foxnews.com/printer_friendly_story/0,3566,60998,00.html.

FR. "Zum Umsturz mag Berlin die Iraner nicht aufrufen. Bundesregierung hofft auf Einlenken Teherans beim Atomprogramm, Zweifel am Einfluss Khatamis wachsen." *Frankfurter Rundschau* 20 June 2003, 6.

Fried, Nico. "Zum Auftakt viel guter Wille; Berlin und Washington suchen Gemeinsamkeiten." *Süddeutsche Zeitung* 1 December 2005, 6.

FT. "Dangerous liaisons in US foreign policy: President Bush's second-term cabinet marches in lockstep." *Financial Times (London)* 20 November 2004, 12.

Gaffney, Frank. "Divest Iran." *Washington Times* 31 May 2006, A16.

Gellman, Barton, and Dafna Linzer. "Unprecedented Peril Forces Tough Calls. President Faces a Multi-Front Battle Against Threats, Known, Unknown." *Washington Post* 26 October 2004, A01.

Gerecht, Reuel Marc. Regime Change in Iran? *American Enterprise Institute*, 1 August 2002 [acessed: 6 April 2006]. Available from http://www.aei.org/publications/pubID.14201/pub_detail.asp.

Germany Info, Press Release. Agreed Statement at the End of a Visit to the Islamic Republic of Iran by the Foreign Ministers of Britain, France And Germany 21 October 2003 [acessed: 16 April 2006]. Available from http://www.germany.info/relaunch/info/press/releases/pr_10_21_03.htm.

Globalsecurity.org. Badr Corps [acessed: 17 May 2006]. Available from http://www.globalsecurity.org/military/world/para/badr.htm.

Gordon, Philip H. "The Transatlantic Alliance and the International System." In: Conflict and Cooperation in Transatlantic Relations, edited by Daniel Hamilton, Washington, D.C.: SAIS Center for Transatlantic Relations, 2004: 75-84.

Graham, Bradley. "U.S. Officials Discout Risk of Iran-Style Rule." *Washington Post* 7 February 2005, A18.

Grant, Charles. "The Decline of American Power." *CER Bulletin*, Issue 29 (April/May 2003).

Gvosdev, Nicholas. Crisis of American Power: Layne, Tucker, Hendrickson *The Washington Realist*, 1 August 2006 [acessed: 12 September 2006]. Available from http://washingtonrealist.blogspot.com/2006/08/crisis-of-american-power-layne-tucker.html.

Harnden, Toby. "US accuses Syria and Iran of 'hostile acts'." *Telegraph* 29 March 2003.

Hermann, Charles F. "Changing Course: When Governments Choose to Redirect Foreign Policy." *International Studies Quarterly*, 34, 3 (1990): 3-21.

Hersh, Seymour M. Fact: The Coming Wars. What the Pentagon can now do in secret *The New Yorker*, 24 January 2005 [acessed: 31 May 2005. Available from http://www.newyorker.com/fact/content/?050124fa_fact.

―――. Fact: The Iran Plans. Would President Bush go to war to stop Tehran from getting the bomb? *The New Yorker*, 17 April 2006 [acessed: 31 May 2006. Available from http://www.newyorker.com/fact/content/articles/060417fa_fact.

Hoagland, Jim. "Iran's Gift: New Unity in the West." *Washington Post* 23 February 2006, A19.

Howard, Roger. EU3-Iran Deal Exposes Underlying International Tensions *Royal United Services Institute for Defence and Security Studies (RUSI)*, December 2004 [acessed: 3 February 2006]. Available from http://www.rusi.org/forward.php?structureID=S4058647E8B76D&ref=P41BD74CDB2209&sho wall=&print=true.

Hulsman, John C. Beyond the neocons: ethical realism and America's future *Opendemocracy.com*, 21 September 2006 [acessed: 23 September 2006]. Available from http://www.opendemocracy.net/democracy-americanpower/neocons_3925.jsp.

―――. "Bush's home run: neocon victory, realist world." *Opendemocracy.com*, (23 November 2004).

Hulsman, John C., and James Philips. "Forging a common transatlantic approach to the Iranian nuclear problem." *Heritage Foundation Backgrounder*, 1837 (23 March 2005).

Ikenberry, G. John. "America's Imperial Ambition." *Foreign Affairs*, 82, September/October (2002).

―――, ed. *America Unrivaled. The Future of the Balance of Power, Cornell Studies in Security Affairs.* Ithaca: Cornell University Press, 2002.

IRNA. Iran rejects preconditions for nuclear talks 20 August 2006 [acessed: 12 September 2006]. Available from http://www.irna.ir/en/news/view/line-24/0608201710152643.htm.

Joffe, Josef. Oil, Sweat and Fears. While containing and deterring Iran, there is time for talks *Atlantic Times*, May 2006 [acessed: 10 June 2006]. Available from http://www.atlantic-times.com/archive_detail.php?recordID=492.

Johnson, Jo, and Gareth Smyth. "Europe trio seeks guarantee on Iran nuclear policy." *Financial Times (London)* 30 July 2004, 11.

Kagan, Robert. "On Iran, Giving Futility Its Chance." *Washington Post* 13 July 2006, A23.

―――. "Power and Weakness." *Policy Review*, June & July (2002): 3-28.

Kamp, Karl-Heinz. "Von der Prävention zur Präemption? Die neue amerikanische Sicherheitsstrategie." *Internationale Politik*, 12/2002 (2002): 19-24.

Kaplan, Lawrence F. "Tehran Twist - Bush's New Iran Policy." *The New Republic*, 28 March 2005.

Kemp, Geoffrey. Iran and Iraq: The Shia Connection, Soft Power, and the Nuclear Factor *United States Institute of Peace*, November 2005 [accessed: 13 March 2006]. Available from http://www.usip.org/pubs/specialreports/sr156.html.

Keohane, Robert O. *International Institutions and State Power*, Boulder: Westview, 1989.

─────, ed. *Neorealism and its Critics*. New York: Columbia University Press, 1986.

Kessler, Glenn. "Impact From the Shadows. Cheney Wields Power With Few Fingerprints." *Washington Post* 5 October 2004, A01.

─────. "Iran Warned, but Russia, China Dissent on Action." *Washington Post* 31 March 2006, A16.

─────. "Rice Asks for $75 Million to Increase Pressure on Iran." *Washington Post* 16 February 2006, A01.

─────. "Rice Key to Reversal on Iran; Expected Failure of International Effort Led to U.S. Turnaround." *Washington Post* 4 June 2006, A17.

─────. "Rice Taps Longtime Colleagues for Inner Circle." *Washington Post* 7 June 2005, A21.

─────. "Shift in U.S. Stance Shows Power of Seven-Letter Word." *Washington Post*, 1 June 2006, A13.

─────. "U.S. Eyes Pressing Uprising In Iran; Officials Cite Al Qaeda Links, Nuclear Program." *Washington Post* 25 May 2003, A01.

─────. "U.S. Has Shifting Script on N. Korea; Administration Split as New Talks Near." *Washington Post* 7 December 2003, A25.

Kessler, Glenn, and Peter Slevin. "Rice Fails to Repair Rifts, Officials Say; Cabinet Rivalries Complicate Her Role." *Washington Post* 12 October 2003, A01.

Kessler, Glenn, and Robin Wright. "Edwards Says Kerry Plans To Confront Iran On Weapons." *Washingon Post* 30 August 2004, A01.

Kohut, Andrew, and Bruce Stokes. *America Against the World: How We Are Different And Why We Are Disliked*, New York: Times Books, 2006.

Koppel, Ted. Cheney Wields Unprecedented V.P. Power. On Iraq and Elsewhere, Many Say Cheney Wields New Vice-Presidential Clout *ABC News*, 29 November 2003 [acessed: 12 May 2006]. Available from http://abcnews.go.com/Nightline/story?id=129012.

Kornblut, Anne E. "Bush Hears Endorsement From Schroder About Iran." *New York Times* 28 June 2005, A12.

Krasner, Stephen D. "Power, Polarity, and the Challenge of Disintegration." In: America and Europe in an Era of Change, edited by Helga Haftendorn and Christian Tuschoff, Boulder: Westview Press, 1993: 21-42.

Krell, Gert. *Weltbilder und Weltunordnung. Einführung in die Theorie der Internationalen Beziehungen.* 3rd ed., Baden-Baden: Nomos, 2004.

Labott, Elise. Armitage, Bolton often clashed, aide says. Says U.N. nominee a source of tension at State Department *CNN.com*, 10 May 2005 [accessed: 7 May 2006]. Available from http://www.cnn.com/2005/POLITICS/05/10/bolton.armitage/index.html.

LaFranchi, Howard. "A bid to foment democracy in Iran." *Christian Science Monitor* 17 February 2006, 3.

Lake, Anthony. "Confronting Backlash States." *Foreign Affairs*, 74, 2, March/April (1994): 45-55.

Landler, Mark. "Nuclear Agency Votes to Report Iran to U.N. Security Council for Treaty Violation." *New York Times* 25 September 2005, 6.

————. "U.N. Atom Agency Gives Iran Both a Slap and a Pass." *New York Times* 27 November 2003, A22.

Lane, Charles. "Germany's New Ostpolitik." *Foreign Affairs*, 74, 6, November/December (1994): 77-89.

Ledeen, Michael. Is Bill Clinton Still President? *National Review Online*, 7 June 2006 [accessed: 8 June 2006]. Available from http://article.nationalreview.com/?q=ZDg2YzE3ZGQwYWVmYjQ2MDBhZmU0N2NiMzcxYm U2ZGGQ=.

Lehmkuhl, Ursula. *Theorien Internationaler Politik. Einführung und Texte.* 3rd ed., München: R. Oldenbourg Verlag, 2001.

Leithäuser, Johannes. "Die EU will den Iran-Konflikt in den Sicherheitsrat bringen." *Frankfurter Allgemeine Zeitung* 13 January 2006, 1.

————. "Eine oft vorgetragene Frage. Berlin hat Washington zu Verhandlungen mit Teheran aufgefordert." *Frankfurter Allgemeine Zeitung* 2 June 2006, 5.

Leverett, Flynt L. "Iran: The Gulf Between Us." *New York Times* 24 January 2006, A21.

Lexington. "Hard-line and soft-line in foreign policy." *The Economist* 23 October 2003.

————. United States Foreign Policy: The Shadow Men *The Economist*, 24 April 2003 [accessed: 12 June 2006]. Available from http://www.economist.com/world/na/displayStory.cfm?story_id=1731327.

Lieven, Anatol, and John Hulsman. *Ethical Realism: A Vision for America's Role in the World*, New York: Pantheon, 2006.

————. The Folly Of Exporting Democracy *TomPaine.com*, 12 September 2006 [accessed: 13 September 2006]. Available from http://www.tompaine.com/articles/2006/09/12/the_folly_of_exporting_democracy.php.

Lind, Michael. Is America the New Roman Empire? *The Globalist*, 19 June 2002 [accessed: 12 June 2006]. Available from http://www.theglobalist.com/DBWeb/StoryId.aspx?StoryId=2526.

Linzer, Dafna. "Allies at IAEA Meeting Reject U.S. Stand on Iran; Draft Asks for Suspension of Nuclear Work." *Washington Post* 18 September 2004, A22.

————. "Bolton Often Blocked Information, Officials Say. Iran, IAEA Matters Were Allegedly Kept From Rice, Powell." *Washington Post* 18 April 2005, A04.

————. "Bush Cautiously Optimistic as Iran Offers to Negotiate." *Washington Post* 10 August 2005, A11.

————. "IAEA Leader's Phone Tapped. U.S. Pores Over Transcripts to Try to Oust Nuclear Chief." *Washington Post* 12 December 2004, A01.

———. "Iran Negotiates Deal to Curtail Nuclear Work; U.S. Sees Offer as Bid to Stall Sanctions." *Washington Post* 8 September 2004, A14.

———. "Iran Resumes Uranium Work, Ignores Warning." *Washington Post* 9 August 2005, A10.

———. "Iran Says It Will Renew Nuclear Efforts." *Washington Post* 25 June 2004, A01.

———. "No Progress in Nuclear Talks with Iran; U.N. Discussions Likely After European Effort, Powell Says." *Washington Post* 30 July 2004, A14.

———. "Nuclear Agency Praises Iran; IAEA Supports Arms Pact, Won't Seek Sanctions." *Washington Post* 30 November 2004, A01.

———. "U.N. Finds No Nuclear Bomb Program in Iran; Agency Report and Tehran's Deal With Europe Undercut Thougher U.S. Stance." *Washington Post* 16 November 2004, A18.

———. "U.N. Finds No Nuclear Bomb Program in Iran; Agency Report and Tehran's Deal With Europe Undercut Tougher U.S. Stance." *Washington Post* 16 November 2004, A18.

———. "U.S. Backs Russian Plan To Resolve Iran Crisis." *Washington Post* 19 November 2005, A16.

———. "U.S. Plans New Tool to Halt Spread of Weapons." *Washington Post* 27 June 2005, A01.

———. "U.S. Urges Financial Sanctions on Iran." *Washington Post* 29 May 2006, A01.

Linzer, Dafna, and Colum Lynch. "U.S. Agenda on Iran Lacking Key Support." *Washington Post* 16 September 2005, A26.

Linzer, Dafna, and Peter Slevin. "U.N Agency Rebukes Iran on Nuclear Activity; Broken Promises on Disclosure Cited." *Washington Post* 19 June 2004, A01.

Loeb, Vernon. "As Military Spending Booms, Budget Debate Looms." *Washington Post* 16 February 2003, A19.

Lynn E. Davis, J. Michael Polich, William M. Hix, Michael D. Greenberg, Stephen D. Brady, and Ronald E. Sortor. *Streched Thin: Army Forces for sustained operations*, Santa Monica: RAND Corp., 2005.

MacAskill, Ewen. "Iran's nuclear facility erodes diplomatic victory." *The Guardian (London)* 1 April 2004, 12.

MacAskill, Ewen, Kasra Naji, and Chris McGreal. "UK sets Iran deadline to end nuclear bomb work." *The Guardian (London)* 9 September 2004, 2.

Mann, James. "The next generation seeks a more diplomatic America." *Financial Times (London)* 26 April 2005, 19.

———. *Rise of the Vulcans. The History of Bush's War Cabinet*, New York: Viking Penguin, 2004.

McCombs, Phil. "This Fire This Time; To Some Scholars, Iraq's Just Part of Something Bigger." *Washington Post* 13 April 2003, F01.

Medick-Krakau, Monika. "Außenpolitischer Wandel: Diskussionsstand - Erklärungsansätze - Zwischenergebnisse." In: Außenpolitischer Wandel in theoretischer und vergleichender Perspektive: Die USA und die Bundesrepublik Deutschland, edited by Monika Medick-Krakau, Baden-Baden: Nomos, 1999: 3-31.

Mertins, Silke, and Hubert Wetzel. "EU bindet USA in Atomgespräche mit Iran ein." *Financial Times Deutschland* 13 October 2004, 14.

Milner, Helen V. *Interests, Institutions, and Information. Domestic Politics and International Relations*, Princeton: Princeton University Press, 1997.

Moravcsik, Andrew. "Liberal Theories of International Relations." *Unpublished Working Paper, Princeton University*, (2006).

———. "Taking Preferences Seriously. A Liberal Theory of International Politics." *International Organization*, 51, 4 (1997): 513-553.

Morgenthau, Hans-Joachim. *Politics Among Nations. The Struggle for Power and Peace*, New York: Alfred A. Knopf., 1948.

Müller, Harald. "Nukleare Krisen und transatlantischer Dissens. Amerikanische und europäische Antworten auf aktuelle Probleme der Weiterverbreitung von Kernwaffen." *HSFK Report*. Frankfurt am Main: Hessische Stiftung Friedens- und Konfliktforschung, September 2003.

Norton-Taylor, Richard. "US and Europe row over Iran." *The Guardian (London)* 14 February 2005, 14.

Nye, Joseph S. "The Decline of America's Soft Power." *Foreign Affairs*, 84, May/June (2004).

———. *The Paradox of American Power: Why the World's Only Superpower Cannot Go it Alone*, Oxford: Oxford University Press, 2002.

O'Sullivan, Meghan L. "The Politics of Dismantling Containment." *Washington Quarterly*, 24, 1 (2001): 67-76.

PBS News Hour. Threat From Tehran? 27 May 2003 [acessed: 8 May 2006]. Available from http://www.pbs.org/newshour/bb/middle_east/jan-june03/iran_5-27.html#.

Perelman, Marc. U.S. Officials Are Mulling Iran Strikes, Experts Say *The Forward*, 7 April 2006 [acessed: 9 May 2006]. Available from http://www.forward.com/articles/7616.

Peters, Ingo. "Introduction: Contending Versions and Competing Visions of Transatlantic Relations." In: Transatlantic Tug-of-War. Prospects for US-European Cooperation. Festschrift in Honor of Helga Haftendorn, edited by Ingo Peters, Münster: Lit-Verlag (forthcoming), 2006.

Peterson, Scott. Why Iran sees no rush for a nuke deal *Christian Science Monitor*, 2006 [acessed: 7 September 2006]. Available from http://www.csmonitor.com/2006/0907/p06s02-wome.html.

Phillips, James, John C. Hulsman, and James Jay Carafano. "Countering Iran's Nuclear Challenge." *Backgrounder*. Washington, DC: The Heritage Foundation, December 14, 2005.

Pollack, Kenneth M. *The Persian Puzzle. The Conflict between Iran and America*, New York: Random House, 2005.

Pond, Elizabeth. *Friendly Fire. The Near-Death of the Transatlantic Alliance*, Washington, D.C.: Brookings Institution Press, 2004.

Priest, Dana. "Iran's Emerging Nuclear Plant Poses Test for U.S." *Washington Post* 29 July 2002, A01.

Proissl, Wolfgang. "Unwiderstehliches Angebot; Nur wenn Deutschland, Frankreich und Großbritannien mit Russland und den USA kooperieren, können sie Irans Atomprogramm ohne Krieg stoppen." *Financial Times Deutschland* 16 September 2004, 35.

Rabinovich, Abraham. "Sale of 'bunker busters' seen as a warning to Iran." *Washington Times* 29 April 2005, A16.

Rice, Condoleezza. Press Conference on Iran *State Department*, 31 May 2006 [acessed: 1 June 2006]. Available from http://www.state.gov/secretary/rm/2006/67103.htm.

————. "Rice optimistic about Bush's bold agenda in his second term, partial transcript of Secretary of State Condoleezza Rice's interview with editors and reporters." *Washington Times* 12 March 2005, A07.

Richelson, Jeffrey. Presidential Directives on National Security from Truman to George W. Bush Volume II *Digital National Security Archive*, [acessed: 12 June 2006]. Available from http://nsarchive.chadwyck.com/pdessayx.htm.

Richter, Paul. "Bush, Merkel United On Iran." *Los Angeles Times* 14 January 2006.

Riecke, Henning. *The Most Ambitious Agenda. Amerikanische Diplomatie gegen die Entstehung neuer Kernwaffenstaaten und das Nukleare Nichtverbreitungsregime*, 2006, *Digitale Dissertation*: Freie Universität Berlin, 2002.

Risen, James, and David Johnston. "Spy Case Renews Debate Over Pro-Israel Lobby's Ties to Conservatives at Pentagon." *New York Times* 4 September 2004, 10.

Risse-Kappen, Thomas. *Cooperation Among Democracies. The European Influence on U.S. Foreign Policy*, Princeton: Princeton University Press, 1995.

Rogers, Paul. "Iran: Consequences of a War." *Briefing Paper*. Oxford: Oxford Research Group, February 2006.

Rohani, Hassan. Iran's Nuclear Program: The Way Out *Time*, 9 May 2006 [acessed: 6 June 2006]. Available from http://www.time.com/time/world/printout/0,8816,1192435,00.html.

Rothkopf, David J. "Look Who's Running the World Now." *Washington Post* 12 March 2006, B01.

————. *Running the World. The Inside Story of the National Security Council and the Architects of American Power*, New York: PublicAffairs, 2005.

Rozen, Laura. "U.S. Moves to Weaken Iran." *Los Angeles Times* 19 May 2006, A6.

Rüb, Mathias. "Washingtons weiter Weg in der Iran-Politik." *Frankfurter Allgemeine Zeitung* 2 June 2006, 5.

Rüb, Matthias. "Fischer bekräftigt Forderung nach Sitz im Sicherheitsrat; Abschluß des UN-Gipfels in New York; Treffen der EU-3 mit iranischem Präsidenten." *Frankfurter Allgemeine Zeitung* 17 September 2005, 1.

————. "Senat bestätigt die Ernennung von Condoleezza Rice." *Frankfurter Allgemeine Zeitung* 27 January 2005, 4.

Rudolf, Peter. "Stigmatisierung bestimmter Staaten. Europa bevorzugt den Dialog." *Internationale Politik*, 6 (1999): 15-22.

Rudolf, Peter, and Geoffrey Kemp. "The Iranian Dilemma. Challenges for German and American Foreign Policy." Washington, DC: AICGS, 1997.

Rüesch, A. "USA für mehr Druck auf Iran im Atomstreit." *Neue Zürcher Zeitung* 20 November 2003, 3.

Sandschneider, Eberhard. "Die USA als dominierende Weltmacht." In: Jahrbuch Internationale Politik 2003/2004, edited by Helmut Hubel, Karl Kaiser, Hanns W. Maull, Eberhard Sandschneider, Klaus-Werner Schatz and Wolfgang Wagner, München: R. Oldenbourg Verlag, 2005: 1-10.

———. "Reinventing Transatlantic Relations." *AICGS/DAAD Working Paper Series*. Washington, DC: AICGS, 2003.

Sanger, David E. "Bush Says U.S. Will Not Tolerate Building of Nuclear Arms by Iran." *New York Times* 19 June 2003, A1.

———. "Cheney Says Israel Might 'Act First' on Iran." *New York Times* 21 January 2005, A6.

———. For Bush, Talks With Iran Were a Last Resort *New York Times*, 1 June 2006 [acessed: 1 June 2006]. Available from http://www.nytimes.com/2006/06/01/world/middleeast/01iran.html?ex=1306814400en=3b4110 3c1ecf3a8eei=5088partner=rssnytemc=rss&pagewanted=print.

———. "Who'd Be In, Who'd Be Out." *New York Times* 17 October 2004.

Sanger, David E., and Steven R. Weisman. "Bush seeks to end turf wars on security issues." *International Herald Tribune* 18 November 2004, 2.

———. "Cabinet Choices Seen as Move For More Harmony and Control." *New York Times* 16 November 2004, A1.

Schmitt, Eric. "Pentagon Office in Spying Case Was Focus of Iran Debate." *New York Times* 2 September 2004, A17.

Schneider, Gerald, and Patricia A. Weitsman. "Eliciting Collaboration From „Risky" States: The Limits of Conventional Multilateralism in Security Affairs." *Global Society*, 11, 1 (January 1997): 93-110.

Schröder, Gerhard. Speech on the 41th Munich Conference on Security Policy 12 February 2005 [acessed: 14 May 2006]. Available from http://www.securityconference.de.

Sciolino, Elaine, and Steven R. Weisman. "U.S. Compromises on Wording of Iran Nuclear Resolution." *New York Times* 4 February 2006, A6.

Sick, Gary. "The US Offer to Iran." *American Iranian Council - AIC Update*, 3, 45 (June 2006).

Skiba, Alexander, and Stephen F. Szabo. "Merkel in Washington, Part Deux." *AICGS Advisor*, 28 April (2006).

Stritzel, Holger. "German and American Perceptions of 'Rogue States'." *AICGS Advisor*, 13 October (2006).

Szabo, Stephen F. *Parting Ways. The crisis in German-American Relations*, Washington, DC: Brookings Press, 2005.

The Economist. Iran, Libya and nukes 13 March 2004 [acessed: 12 May 2006]. Available from http://www.economist.com/world/africa/displaystory.cfm?story_id=E1_NVDPDGN.

The President of the United States of America. "The National Security Strategy of the United States of America." Washington, D.C.: The White House, September 2002.

The White House. *The National Security Strategy of the United States of America*, Washington, D.C., March 2006.

———. President Bush and Chancellor Schröder Discuss Partnership 23 February 2005 [acessed: 12 May 2006]. Available from http://www.whitehouse.gov/news/releases/2005/02/print/20050223-4.html.

————. President Bush Discusses Freedom in Iraq and Middle East Remarks by the President at the 20th Anniversary of the National Endowment for Democracy 6 November 2003 [acessed: 20 April 2006]. Available from http://www.whitehouse.gov/news/releases/2003/11/20031106-2.html.

————. President Delivers Commencement Address at the United States Military Academy at West Point, Mitchie Stadium, United States Military Academy at West Point 27 May 2006 [acessed: 5 June 2006]. Available from http://www.whitehouse.gov/news/releases/2006/05/20060527-1.html.

————. President Discusses the Future of Iraq, Speech before the American Enterprise Institute 26 February 2003 [acessed: 13 June 2006]. Available from http://www.whitehouse.gov/news/releases/2003/02/20030226-11.html.

————. President Sworn-In to Second Term (Inaugural Address 2005) 20 January 2005 [acessed: 7 April 2006]. Available from http://www.whitehouse.gov/news/releases/2005/01/20050120-1.html.

————. President's Remarks to the Press Pool, Brooks County Airport, Falfurrias, Texas 1 January 2004 [acessed: 7 April 2006]. Available from http://www.whitehouse.gov/news/releases/2004/01/20040101.html.

————. Remarks by the President at the United States Air Force Academy Graduation Ceremony 22 June 2004 [acessed: 5 May 2005]. Available from http://www.whitehouse.gov/news/releases/2004/06/20040602.html.

————. Remarks by the Press Secretary on Iran 21 October 2003 [acessed: 13 June 2006]. Available from http://www.whitehouse.gov/news/releases/2003/10/20031021-15.html.

————. Roundtable Interview of the President by the Press Pool, Aboard Air Force One, En Route Canberra, Australia 22 October 2003 [acessed: 4 May 2006]. Available from http://www.whitehouse.gov/news/releases/2003/10/20031022-7.html.

————. State of the Union Address by the President 2 February 2005 [acessed: 8 June 2006]. Available from http://www.whitehouse.gov/news/releases/2005/02/20050202-11.html.

————. State of the Union Address by the President 31 January 2006 [acessed: 1 February 2006]. Available from http://www.whitehouse.gov/stateoftheunion/2006/index.html.

Thränert, Oliver. "Iran Before the Security Council? German Perspectives and Goals." *SWP Comments*. Stiftung Wissenschaft und Politik, 2006.

Times Online. Leaked letter in full: UK diplomat outlines Iran strategy 22 March 2006 [acessed: 23 March 2006]. Available from http://www.timesonline.co.uk/article/0,,2-2098203,00.html.

Traynor, Ian. "Europe's nuclear deal with Iran faces collapse." *The Guardian (London)* 14 February 2004, 16.

U.S. *Department of State*. The Bush Administration's Nonproliferation Policy: Successes and Future Challenges. John R. Bolton, Under Secretary for Arms Control and International Security, Testimony Before the House International Relations Committee 30 March 2004 [acessed: 3 June 2006]. Available from http://www.state.gov/t/us/rm/31029.htm.

————. Interview by The Washington Post 1 October 2003 [acessed: 13 June 2006]. Available from http://www.state.gov/secretary/former/powell/remarks/2003/25139.htm.

Verenkotte, Clemens. *Das Ende der friedlichen Gesellschaft. Deutschlands Illusionen im globalen Krieg*, München: Droemer/Knaur, 2005.

Vick, Karl, and Dafna Linzer. "Iran Requests Direct Talks on Nuclear Program." *Washington Post* 24 May 2006, A01.

Vick, Karl, and Colum Lynch. "No Proposals in Iranian's Letter to Bush, U.S. Says." *Washington Post* 9 May 2006, A18.

Walt, Stephen M. "Containing Rogues and Renegades: Coalition Strategies and Counterproliferation." In: The Coming Crisis. Nuclear Proliferation, U.S. Interests, and World Order, edited by Victor A. Utgoff, Cambridge/London: MIT Press, 2000: 191-226.

———. *The Origins of Alliances*, Ithaca: Cornell University Press, 1987.

Waltz, Kenneth N. *Theory of International Politics*, Reading: Addison-Wesley, 1979.

Weisman, Steven R. "Allies Resist U.S. Efforts to Pressure Iran on Arms." *New York Times* 9 September 2004, A13.

———. "As Iraq was escalates, so does anxiety over Iran." *International Herald Tribune* 21 September 2004, 1.

———. "Bush Aides Divided on Confronting Iran Over A-Bomb." *New York Times* 21 September 2004, A3.

———. "Bush Confronts New Challenge On Issue of Iran." *New York Times* 19 November 2004, A1.

———. "Pressed By U.S., European Banks Limit Iran Deals." *New York Times* 22 May 2006, A1.

———. "Threats and Responses: Washington; U.S. Demands that Iran Turn Over Qaeda Agents and Join Saudi Inquiry." *New York Times* 25 May 2003, A9.

———. "U.S. Accepts Draft on Iran that Omits Use of Force." *New York Times* 31 May 2006, A10.

———. "U.S. Acquiesces in European Plan for Talks With Iran." *New York Times* 16 October 2004, A7.

———. "U.S. acquiesces to allies on new Iran resolution; Nuclear issue will not be referred to UN." *New York Times* 26 November 2003, 3.

———. "U.S. and Allies Court Russia and China to Help Curb Iran." *New York Times* 7 January 2006, A5.

———. "U.S. and Europe Are at Odds, Again, This Time Over Iran." *New York Times* 12 December 2004, A8.

———. "U.S. and Europe delay bid to refer Iran to UN." *International Herald Tribune* 24 November 2005, 6.

———. "U.S. chafes at slow pace of nuclear diplomacy." *International Herald Tribune* 28 March 2005, 1.

———. "U.S. Expands Aid to Iran's Democracy Advocates Abroad." *New York Times* 29 May 2005, 8.

———. "U.S. in Talks With Europeans on a Nuclear Deal With Iran." *New York Times* 12 October 2004, A12.

———. "U.S. Reviewing European Proposal for Iran." *New York Times* 28 February 2005, A6.

———. "Wider U.S. Net Seek Allies Against Iran's Nuclear Plan." *New York Times* 10 September 2005, A3.

Weisman, Steven R., and Judy Dempsey. "Rice works to bolster ties with Europe; She tries to assuage fears U.S. has any plans to attack Iran." *International Herald Tribune* 5 February 2005, 1.

Weisman, Steven R., and David E. Sanger. "U.S. and Britain Try a New Track on Iran." *New York Times* 4 December 2005, 14.

Welt.de. Steinmeier drängt USA zu direkten Gesprächen mit Teheran *Die Welt*, 4 April 2006 [acessed: 12 June 2006]. Available from http://www.welt.de/data/2006/04/04/869750.html.

Wernicke, Christian. "EU-Staaten hoffen auf US-Signal gegenüber Teheran." *Süddeutsche Zeitung* 14 December 2004, 6.

―――. "Knüppel oder Karotte; Europa und Amerika wollen Iran mit "Zuckerbrot und Peitsche" von Atomplänen abbringen." *Süddeutsche Zeitung* 15 October 2004, 6.

Wetzel, Hubert. "Europa drängt USA zu Dialog mit Iran; Im Atomstreit könnte Washington ausreichende Sicherheitsgarantien bieten." *Financial Times Deutschland* 5 April 2006, 15.

Wilkerson, Lawrence B. The White House Cabal 25 October 2005 [acessed: 12 June 2006]. Available from http://www.latimes.com/news/opinion/commentary/la-oe-wilkerson25oct25,0,7455395.story?coll=la-news-comment-opinions.

Winter, Martin. "Die Koalition der Unsicheren." *Süddeutsche Zeitung* 22 April 2006, 9.

Woodward, Bob. *Bush at War*, New York: Simon & Schuster, 2002.

―――. *Plan of Attack*, New York: Simon & Schuster, 2004.

―――. "Should He Stay? The biggest question mark was Secretary of Defense Donald H. Rumsfeld." *Washington Post* 2 October 2006, A01.

―――. *State of Denial: Bush at War, Part III*, New York: Simon & Schuster, 2006.

Wright, Robin. "Bush Weighs Offers to Iran; U.S. Might Join Effort to Halt Nuclear Program." *Washington Post* 28 February 2005, A01.

―――. "Europeans to Press Iran on Nuclear Plans; U.S. Backs Initiative Endorsed by G8 but Is Skeptical Tehran Will Honor Terms." *Washington Post* 16 October 2004, A18.

―――. "Iranian Envoy a Guest of Congress; Similar Visit was Blocked in 2002." *Washington Post* 29 January 2004, A17.

―――. "Rice Says U.S. Won't Join Europe in Iran Nuclear Talks." *Washington Post* 3 February 2005, A10.

―――. "U.S. and Europe Gird for Hard Line From Iran's President." *Washington Post* 26 June 2005, A17.

―――. "U.S. Faces a Crossroads on Iran Policy." *Washington Post* 19 July 2004, A09.

―――. "U.S. In 'Useful' Talks with Iran. The meetings have focused recently on Iraq, Middle East peace efforts and terrorism." *Los Angeles Times* 13 May 2003, 4.

―――. "U.S. Makes Overture To Iran. Sen. Dole Could Head Aid Mission." *Washington Post* 2 January 2004, A01.

―――. "U.S. Wants Guarantees on Iran Effort; Support for U.N. Action Sought if Tehran Does Not Abandon Nuclear Program." *Washington Post* 4 March 2005, A12.

―――. "U.S. Warms to Prospect of New Talks with Iran." *Washington Post* 30 December 2003, A01.

————. "U.S., Allies May Have to Wait Out Iran's Presidential Vote." *Washington Post* 13 March 2005, A16.

————. "U.S., France Warn Iran On Nuclear Program." *Washington Post* 15 October 2005, A11.

Wright, Robin, and Peter Baker. "U.S. to Back Europeans on Incentives for Iran; Rice to Announce Shift on Nuclear Issue." *Washington Post* 11 March 2005, A14.

Wright, Robin, and Michael A. Fletcher. "Bush Denounces Iran's Elections; President Vows to Stand by Citizenry in Struggle for Freedom." *Washington Post* 17 June 2005, A18.

www.ingramcontent.com/pod-product-compliance
Lightning Source LLC
Chambersburg PA
CBHW072152020426
42334CB00018B/1971